FIFE COUNCIL LIBRARIES

Please re

KII   N
G/   CK

D

WITHDRAWN
FROM STOCK

WITHDRAWN
FROM STOCK

F

D1389046

101 Extraordinary Investments

Curious, Unusual and Bizarre Ways to Make Money

FIFE COUNCIL LIBRARIES	
HJ357802	
Askews & Holts	20-Dec-2013
332.63 WAL	£12.99
WORK	KY

HARRIMAN HOUSE LTD
3A Penns Road
Petersfield
Hampshire
GU32 2EW
GREAT BRITAIN

Tel: +44 (0)1730 233870
Fax: +44 (0)1730 233880

Email: enquiries@harriman-house.com
Website: www.harriman-house.com

First published in Great Britain in 2009 by Harriman House. Copyright © Harriman House Ltd
The right of Toby Walne to be identified as the author has been asserted in accordance with the Copyright, Design and Patents Act 1988.

ISBN 978-1-906659-25-7

British Library Cataloguing in Publication Data. A CIP catalogue record for this book can be obtained from the British Library. All rights reserved; no part of this publication may be reproduced, stored in a retrieval system, or transmitted in any form or by any means, electronic, mechanical, photocopying, recording, or otherwise without the prior written permission of the Publisher.

This book may not be lent, resold, hired out or otherwise disposed of by way of trade in any form of binding or cover other than that in which it is published without the prior written consent of the Publisher.

Every effort has been made to obtain permission for the use of all images. Any omissions will be rectified in the next edition.

No responsibility for loss occasioned to any person or corporate body acting or refraining to act as a result of reading material in this book can be accepted by the Publisher, by the Author, or by the employer of the Author.

Printed in the UK by CPI William Clowes, Beccles NR34 7TL.

101 Extraordinary Investments

Curious, Unusual and Bizarre Ways to Make Money

A handbook for the adventurous collector

Discovered & explored by

Toby Walne

Sacha, Sophia & Harrison

Contents

Introduction

'Dr Livingstone, I presume?'

Adventurer and journalist Henry Morton Stanley asked this simple question upon discovering the seriously ill explorer on the shores of Lake Tanganyika, in the remote African settlement of Ujiji in October 1871.

'Yes, and I feel thankful that I am here to welcome you,' came the stiff-upper-lipped response.

The quote is part of the legend of Victorian exploration. Whether it was actually said or not is open to debate. But the spirit of adventure embodied in this event, as well as some remarkable and largely unknown facts surrounding it, certainly mark the inspiration for this book.

It was a golden era of discovery when the sun never set on the British Empire.

Dr David Livingstone had returned from the earlier, ill-fated Zambezi Expedition in 1864. This government-backed trip to Africa had utterly failed in its objective to navigate the fourth-longest river of the "Dark Continent". The Scottish former missionary was pilloried for leading such a hopeless quest. His reputation was ruined and a promising career as an explorer seemingly finished.

Yet two years later he was back searching for the source of the Nile.

How on earth was such a feat possible?

Livingstone's reputation was destroyed but his business mind was not. He was among the first to realise the great financial rewards open to those who could cater to a new breed of investors who might fund adventurous ideas.

He had returned with a number of curious artefacts, including tribal relics and rare species of orchid. As a fellow of the Royal Geographical Society he enjoyed unprecedented access to other adventurers, scientists as well as financiers – men who would also become investors, given the right objects, curios and discoveries to invest in.

Among this closely-knit community in time was the very same Henry Morton Stanley, who not only provided the famous quote but was also the first person to travel the full length of the Congo River. Others included Charles Darwin and fellow African adventurers John Hanning Speke and Richard Francis Burton. In the Edwardian era they were joined by a new generation, including Robert Falcon Scott and Ernest Shackleton.

Exploration funds were often simply raised by trading in curiosities picked up on travels – from shrunken heads used as a currency in Papua New Guinea, to African chieftain masks, Amazonian butterflies, and colonial postage stamps.

Unfortunately, because of a rigid code of honour, many of these trades were conducted in secret, within the confines of an inner circle. Few records survive of the various deals undertaken behind the oak-panelled interiors of exclusive gentlemen's clubs, tucked away in London's Mayfair, or carried out in the hallways of mysterious lodges.

What is not commonly known is that this business is still very much alive and thriving today hidden by the very same – as well as many other – closed doors, with a wide range of modern collectables changing hands along with traditional and unusual curiosities.

Yet times are changing. During this difficult financial climate it seems right to open up to all, at last, the secret world of extraordinary investments. For the world of alternative investments has greatly expanded and greatly altered over time. Although classic artefacts still remain firm favourites, you no longer have to be a prodigiously mustachioed gentleman explorer to participate, or make money, in this game.

With the publishing of this book, many of the modern "adventurers" who have reaped the benefits to regale their exploits over drinks by a roaring fire – occasionally also observed by exotic conquests on the wall – may be alarmed.

And the establishment fat cats and financial advisers who profit from our stock market punts and from devilish derivative products – in the misguided name of "traditional investments" – should also fear the revelation of each item.

This is because many of these opportunities have been well guarded as secrets.

But be warned. No investment is without risk – it is part of the white-knuckle voyage of discovery. The privileged information within this book requires genuine interest and an understanding that values can go down as well as up.

Yet never forget to partake at all times in the derring-do spirit of Victorian adventure. The day belongs to the brave and the bold.

Accept my warmest of welcomes to the inner sanctum of extraordinary investments. I hope you will enjoy the fun and excitement of exploring these many curious and unusual ways to make money.

Let the adventure begin...

Action Man

Action Man is making a comeback not just as a toy but also as a shrewd investment.

Nostalgia is feeding the market among grown-up boys who enjoyed Action Man in their childhood and want to go on adventures with him again (or perhaps share the thrills with a younger generation). In the past few years original action figures made from 1966 onwards have typically been rising in value by about 5% a year, with the earliest models now worth as much as £600.

Action Man also has a wardrobe that can be even more collectable than the doll. Among the hundreds of garments, the most valuable is a Seventies cricket strip so rare that collectors can pay as much as £6000 for it. Another highly sought after costume is an early Green Beret uniform that can fetch £3000.

Action Man was honourably discharged from duty in 1984 when youngsters started buying Star Wars figures instead, and this has helped push up his collectable value.

He came back in 1996 as a less appealing cartoon-like toy, having undertaken his training at a boot camp run by brain-storming toy salesmen rather than a sergeant major on parade. These later dolls are worthless.

Action Man began life as an American citizen – GI Joe – in 1964, before emigrating to Britain two years later.

The livid scar on the right cheek is a birthmark. It was not caused by a fighting accident but is a stamp of authenticity. Another quirk is the right hand thumbnail being on the palm side of the thumb on all figures.

Action Man, unlike his imitators, has always had 20 moveable body parts.

HAIR TODAY...

The first fuzzy haired Action Man soldier came out in 1970. The hairpiece came from an invention earlier shown on TV's *Tomorrow's World*. Some grew a beard from 1971. The rubber-gripped hands were not introduced until 1973.

As with other collectables, it is the models that have not actually been played with but kept in pristine condition (firmly inside their original boxes, with instructions) that are the ones sought after by enthusiasts – it more than doubles their value.

Getting the combat soldier ready for duty in full battle dress is not always easy, as the complete uniform typically comes from several separately available accessories. Among the hardest to find is the entrenching tool – often broken when mistakenly opened without the safety screw first being unscrewed. This is just one of the highly sought after and valuable accessories of Action Man.

In a chequered military history, as well as fighting in the British Army, Navy and Royal Air Force, he has been known to fight for the other side. He was once a German Stormtrooper, and has also been a Russian and French Resistance fighter.

And although under no circumstances afraid of combat, he was never the one to start wars. Clearly a peaceable cove at heart, among his other careers – offered in highly collectable sets that can fetch many hundreds of pounds – are lifeguard, deep-sea diver and football player.

 ## SIGNING UP WITH ACTION MAN

For information on Action Man, including modern vintage action figure copies, contact The Modellers Loft in Caterham, Surrey: www.modellersloft.co.uk. Collectors can trade and share tips on another website called onesixthcollectors.co.uk.

Action Man guide books offering collectable information include *Action Man: The Ultimate Collectors Guide*, by Alan Hall; *On Land, Sea and in the Air: Action Man*, by N. G. Taylor; *Action Man – the Real Story 1966-1996*, by Kevin King; and *Action Man* by Ian Harrison.

Anglepoise Lamp

The Anglepoise lamp can provide an illuminating investment. The springs-and-levers light fell out of fashion in the Eighties when it could be picked up for a few pounds at charity shops. But it has recently been rediscovered as a classic, and now changes hands for up to £400.

The first Anglepoise was the "1208", launched in 1933 with a small shade, two springs and a curved base, and is primarily of interest as a historic artefact rather than a practical investment.

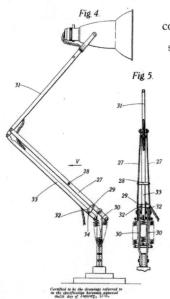

Fig. 4

Fig. 5

Certified to be the drawings referred to in the specification herewith annexed the19 day of January, 19..

Ottawa, Ont., Canada.

This was replaced in 1934 with the iconic and highly collectable "1227", which had three springs, a larger rimmed shade perforated near the top, and an all important square stepping base with three tiers. Examples of the early "1227" lamps are the most sought after, and are often traded for £300 or more. However, even battered lamps can sell for £100.

The Anglepoise lamp was originally intended to help factory workmen focus on handling fiddly components, but after licensing the manufacturing to Herbert Terry & Sons it also became a firm utility favourite for desk top users. The base was reduced to just two tiers in the late Thirties to save on the amount of metal used in production. This later derivation, although still iconic, is less sought after – but is still likely to sell for around £150.

There were also some unusual derivations, including a Lancaster bomber Anglepoise used during WWII by navigators, worth £100. Other spin-offs include Anglepoise mirrors and magnifying glasses.

There have been a few minor changes to the "1227" over the years, among them the lip on the shade disappearing in the Sixties, plus the loss of the stepped base in favour of a rounded finish.

The company recently began making an Anglepoise "Giant 1227" floor lamp that stands 2.7m high. Although only being made in limited numbers, the initial £1900 price tag means it is far too early to say whether these will also go up in value.

A BRIGHT IDEA

The iconic "1227" Anglepoise design was released in 1934 and invented by motor engineer George Carwardine. He had been working on vehicle suspension systems when he came up with a spring that could move in every direction yet remain rigid when held in position. He patented it in 1932 and, inspired by the principle of human limbs, envisioned using it in a lamp.

Authenticity is key. Investors are more interested in a battered and bruised Anglepoise with a sense of history than a pimped-up shiny example that has been renovated. Look at the quality of the springs as these can rust. If they are not working properly it affects how the lamp moves.

Original shades tended to be painted in the traditional black or cream, and occasionally in red, canary yellow, blue, or a camouflage green. The arms were usually the same colour. To hide imperfections, the paint was often not smooth and shiny but mottled with a rough "stone enamel" finish for the shade and base.

The wiring of the old lamps would not pass current regulations so the original old braiding is an authentic touch not required. Also, the bulb holders were made of Bakelite – and bore the maker's logo "Crabtree" – but over time many of these have cracked and are unsafe to use. Modern replacements cost just a few pounds.

 ## SEEKING ILLUMINATION

The Anglepoise official website provides historic information: www.anglepoise.com. Car boot sales, charity shops and auctions still throw up the occasional bargain. Internet trading websites like eBay offer sales, but be wary of paying over the odds for reconditioned lamps.

Antarctic Exploration

The British spirit of adventure is captured at its best in the courage of Edwardian Antarctic explorers. Fighting impossible conditions with a stiff upper lip of steel, staring down death with derring-do valour, the explorers Captain Scott and Ernest Shackleton were an inspiration to the glorious turn-of-the-century Empire. Interest has not dimmed over the past 100 years; prices of relics from their exploits have doubled the auction estimates in recent times and these are continuing to rise.

Captain Robert Falcon Scott led a three-year National Antarctic Expedition in 1901 (actually accompanied by Ernest Shackleton as third officer) on the ship Discovery. They got farther south than anyone had managed before and returned as national heroes.

It wasn't until 1910 that Scott had raised enough funds to tackle the pole again, sailing out this time on the ship Terra Nova. Although ending in failure – being beaten by the underhanded Norwegian Roald Amundsen – the names of Scott, Wilson, Oates,

Bowers and Evans are forever immortalised for the bold and resolutely British way they met their icy deaths.

Diaries that bring adventure to life are most valuable, and a journal by Scott's second-in-command on the 1901 expedition, Captain Albert Armitage, sold for £36,000 in 2004. Manuscripts went for £26,000.

A letter sent to Scott addressed to the Antarctic Post Office by the Royal Geographic Society, which got lost and arrived a year after his death, sold for £43,000 in 2000.

Scott's diary of the later expedition, including the famous 'Great God! This is an awful place,' written in January 1912 on reaching the pole, is considered a national treasure, and held by the British Library.

Any memento of their brave exploits can be an historic keepsake of lasting value. A breakfast biscuit that had belonged to Captain Scott was bought by explorer Sir Ranulph Fiennes for £3900 in 2000, and a sprig of fake holly taken on the expedition for a Christmas pudding sold for £4025. Scott's 1912 snow goggles went under the hammer for £20,700, while a pipe he smoked sold for £8000.

 ## SLEDGE DOGS AND ENGLISHMEN

The British love of dogs played a crucial role in Scott being beaten to the South Pole by Amundsen. Scott man-hauled supplies by sledge – mechanical sledges having failed – believing it was far nobler and less cruel to dogs. Amundsen used dogs to pull sledges, and these could be eaten along the way when food supplies ran low.

Ernest Shackleton had returned to the Antarctic with his own expedition in 1908 on the ship Nimrod. He made it to within 97 miles of the pole before turning back and picking up a knighthood for his endeavours.

But it is the 1914 Antarctic coast-to-coast mission for which he is perhaps best remembered – when his ship, the Endurance, was slowly crushed in ice. It forced the crew on a six month trek to Elephant Island, and then on a perilous 800 mile boat trip to a Norwegian whaling station, where they were rescued against what seemed like impossible odds: 'Not a life lost and we have been through Hell.'

Shackleton's 1908 book *Aurora Australis*, of which only 100 copies were printed, can change hands for £35,000, while original prints taken on the Endurance mission by photographer Frank Hurley are worth at least £50,000.

An Imperial Trans-Antarctic Expedition flag sold for £35,287 in 2000, and the standard went for £64,000. A diary by Endurance doctor Dr Macklin – which describes the ship crushed by ice 'like a huge animal in pain, twisting, shivering, groaning, whining as her timbers gave way before the terrible pressure' – sold for £104,940.

 JOIN THE EXPEDITION

The Antarctic adventures of Scott and Shackleton are covered in numerous books. Start with *Journals: Captain Scott's Last Expedition* by Robert Falcon Scott and Max Jones (Oxford University Press). The Scott Polar Research Institute at Cambridge can be found at www.spri.cam.ac.uk. Auction houses occasionally hold polar expedition sales.

Autographs

The value of the most sought after scribbles have soared almost tenfold over the past decade, transforming a stage door loitering hobby into an exciting opportunity for savvy investors. But if you want to bag a bargain to maximise returns it may still be necessary to stand out in the cold.

The surging market for celebrity signatures also ensures you must confront the biggest of all problems facing autograph hunters – fakes. Enthusiasts not willing to queue should get a full history of the signature and start by only dealing with reputable traders. Internet trading is fraught with dangers for the novice and is a natural home for forgery sharks.

 ## MUCH ADO ABOUT SIGNATURES

The most sought after and difficult to acquire is "The Bard", William Shakespeare. There are only six known examples and none have ever come on the market. They would be worth millions of pounds.

Historical figures tend to be the most valuable. One of the most important is the father of the Parliamentary system Oliver Cromwell, whose signatures cost at least £100,000. Modern historic figures signed much more, but what they put their name to can bump up the value. The big money typically goes for autographed photos, which can command more than four times the price of a straight signature.

A signed photo of Winston Churchill can cost between £1500 and £5000 depending on the iconic nature of the picture. You can pick up Hitler's signature from £2000. More recent historic figures, such as that of first man on the moon Neil Armstrong, have seen their signature values rocket to £3500 from £475 in just a decade.

Hollywood stars are not so predictable because of changes in taste.

Icons such as Steve McQueen and Marlon Brando, who both rarely signed their names, have always had their autograph value grow, and can command prices of at least £1000 if the signature is on a great picture. Yet other icons, such as Betty Davis and Marilyn Monroe, can be picked up for a fraction of this amount, as studios forced them to sign lots of fan mail.

Genre-defining 1940s star Humphrey Bogart costs £600 while a modern-day star can usually be picked up for less than £100. Exceptions are stars that rarely get out their pens and so have a higher rarity value – like Russell Crowe.

The Beatles are top of the pops for music collectables. George Harrison could have been patiently stalked a decade ago for a signature worth £175. This would now go under the hammer for £1500.

Sports stars are among the most prolific signers so their scribbles tend to be worth the least. Exceptions are the biggest names of all, like Muhammad Ali. Signed photos of Pele, for instance, have risen in value from £100 to £800 in just a decade.

Treat the mark of a star with care if you wish to show it off. Many people frame them. Make sure the photo is not touching the glass and the signature is kept out of direct sunlight – otherwise they can be destroyed over time.

SIGNING UP

Industry must-read *The Sanders Price Guide to Autographs* offers price guides. American magazine *Autograph* provides trading tips and information (see www.autographcollector.com). Visit bi-annual Autographica trade fairs in London to meet hunters and dealers for a feel of the market (www.autographica.co.uk).

Automatons

The automaton is not to be mistaken with the robot. It uses non-electronic moving parts to perform independent, self-operated movements, as if acting of its own will. The results are highly collectable, historic pieces of cog-and-spring ingenuity that continue to rise in value.

"The Turk" is the most famous automaton of all – though actually a fake. Built in 1770 by Wolfgang von Kempelen, he toured the courts of Europe astounding guests with a chess-playing machine in the form of a mechanical, turbaned Turk. Hidden behind cogs and levers was a man playing by candlelight. Sadly, it was destroyed in a fire during the 19th century.

Another great piece is the Canard Digerateur – or digesting duck. Invented in 1739 by French engineer Jacques de Vaucanson, it performed the illusion of eating and defecating. Like "The Turk", it was lost in a fire, this time at a Russian museum in 1879.

Another fascinating piece is the now priceless "Tippoo's Tiger", made in 1795 for the Tippoo Sultan of Mysore in India, a model of a British soldier being mauled to death. It performs the sound of growls from the big cat as well as shrieks from the doomed victim and is kept at the Victoria and Albert Museum in London.

The most highly skilled 18th century automaton makers include Frenchman Pierre Jaquet-Droz, Swiss Henri Maillardet and Belgian

John Joseph Merlin. Mechanisms made by their hands can fetch more than £100,000 each.

Later pieces from the late 19th and early 20th century – particularly from France – are also extremely collectable; normal examples can still cost thousands of pounds.

French makers to keep an eye out for include Roullet & Decamps, whose animated figures go for up to £100,000. However, relative bargains are still available and a Roullet & Decamps violin player recently sold for a more affordable £5000.

Another late 19th century collectable is Leopold Lambert. Novelty items by Lambert, such as his "nègre fumeur", or "smoking negro", have sold for £3000, though more elaborate smoking examples accompanied by music have changed hands for £20,000. Bontems is another name to look for, with his singing automaton bird sitting in a tree recently selling for £4000. Gustave Vichy also made collectable and exotic automatons and a Japanese mask seller of his may sell for £10,000.

Other greats include Phalibois and Renou.

LEONARDO DA VINCI

Leonardo da Vinci designed an automaton in the late 15th century. The device could move its arms and legs, and sit up. It was finally built in 1997 by NASA cybernetics experts carefully following his detailed sketches. It was indeed a fully working automaton.

Those with deep enough pockets can still pick up late 18th century examples from one of the masters, such as the Jaquet-Droz musical box with singing bird that recently went at auction for £90,000.

There is also a genre of automata that focuses on watches. These tend to involve hidden compartments opened to reveal tiny pictures of erotic fantasies.

Most of the collectable automaton watches were made in the 17th and 18th century for gentlemen who enjoyed the thrill of risqué scenes hidden away in timepieces. The automaton watches are often unsigned but skilfully made. They sell for thousands of pounds and – like the sex scenes – are always in demand.

AUTOMATON, AND ON AND ON

A good place to start is contemporary automata, which can be picked up for a few hundred pounds from firms like Cabaret Mechanical Theatre (www.cabaret.co.uk). Auction houses hold sales, including Sotheby's (www.sothebys.com).

Bakelite Telephone

Interest in the early 20th century vintage Candlestick handsets, as well as later classic Bakelite designs, have sent prices of the top examples soaring. Phones that were going for £25 a couple of decades ago now fetch ten times this amount and continue to rise in value.

 ## THE FIRST PHONE CALL

'Mr Watson, come here. I want you.' These were the first words ever uttered down a phone line. The sentence came from Scottish-born inventor Alexander Bell in 1876. Bell became a founding member of the National Geographic Society in 1888 and was one of the great Victorian minds. He also refused to have a telephone in his study – it disturbed his work.

In 1924 the 150 Candlestick phone was approved by the British Post Office, forerunner of the General Post Office (GPO). Made of steel, cast iron and brass, with a Bakelite earpiece and separate wooden-cabinet bell, the quality has stood the test of time. Re-serviced Candlestick sets can sell for £400.

Then came the pyramid-shaped 200 series with its iconic design and handsome chunky Bakelite shape. Initially rolled out as a 162 table top model in 1926 it was given an internal makeover – though it still looked the same – with the 232 in 1934. Investors might shell out at least £300 for a reconditioned handset.

The 300 series Bakelite came out in 1937. Although more abundant than earlier phones, the classic 332 model with its practical construction (the first with an internal bell), makes it the most appealing for modern users seeking vintage phone style. It typically changes hands for £150 to £250.

The next model – 706 – was lighter and more plastic feeling, with smoother curves. It began production in 1959. Despite coming in a variety of colours it has yet to capture the imagination of many collectors and handsets can still be picked up for £50.

A wide range of British manufacturers, including British Ericsson, Siemens Brothers, GEC, Plessey and Automatic Telephone Manufacturing, made the vintage Candlestick and Bakelite telephones.

When looking to buy an old phone, the physical condition of the Bakelite is of paramount importance. Chips and cracks are hard to repair and any damage is likely to at least halve the value.

Colour is also a vital factor. The vast majority of phones were black. A standard 332 fetching £200 rises to £350 if ivory, £500 if red, and £800 in Bakelite green, due to escalating rarity. However, get your hands on a black phone with green handset and you may have a "scramble" telephone as used by wartime leader Winston Churchill, worth £1000.

Many early phones had a "cheeseboard" tray that pulled out at the front as a storage place for telephone numbers. Most were replaced, as they tended to jam; but find one intact and it can add £50 to a phone's value.

Derivatives include the 312 with a chrome "call exchange" button for party line sharing, as well as the 314 and 328 which also have buttons to turn the bell off and on. Buttons can add up to £100 to the price.

Originality is vital, but when it comes to the sound quality a modern conversion can enhance the appeal if you don't wish to regularly shout down the phone. It may also be necessary to convert to a standard phone socket.

DIAL THE RIGHT NUMBER

The Telecommunications Heritage Group (www.thg.org.uk); leaflet *Old Telephones* by Andrew Emmerson, £1.75. Traders include Antique Telephones (www.antiquetelephones.co.uk) and The Old Telephone Company (www.theoldtelephone.co.uk).

Barbie Doll

Barbie celebrated her 50th birthday in 2009 but is still a sprightly investment. Collectors who forked out £1.70 for the very first dolls, complete with black-and-white swimsuit, now have an investment worth at least £8000 if she is still enjoying life in her original packaging. Even out of the box the very earliest Barbie fetches £2500 so long as the factory-lacquered hair is still in shape.

The record paid for a Barbie is the £9000 handed over for a pristine 1965 model at a Christie's auction in 2006. Even modern limited edition Barbie dolls produced today have been known to soar as much as ten-fold in value in a year to £300.

Barbie was born in America in 1959 and her full name is Barbara Millicent Roberts – named after the daughter of creators Elliot and Ruth Handler.

Drippy boyfriend Ken, brought out in 1961, is not actually a love interest at all, but modelled on Barbara's brother Ken. This may explain why she has always preferred the company of Action Man to the squeaky clean boy-next-door.

Her origins are not that of a wholesome All-American girl but a sexy German adult woman called Bild Lilli, a racy newspaper comic strip character who wore lacy underwear and stilettos. Ruth Handler saw the Bild Lilli doll while on holiday in Germany during the mid-Fifties and copied it when she went home.

The 1959 Barbie is easy to recognise as she had holes in the bottom of her feet to set her on a stand. (These holes disappeared from 1960 onwards.) She also wore a black-and-white swimsuit and black high-heeled mules.

But the years have not been kind to every early Barbie. Telltale signs to look out for in early models include copper-based earrings, which can oxidise and cause permanent "green ear", plus a sweaty or pale body, from unstable plastics.

For authenticity check out the right cheek of Barbie's bottom for a date stamp. But be wary as the market is awash with "Frankenstein fakes", figures made up of parts from different dolls, meaning that expert help should be sought when handing over serious money.

Barbie has gone under the plastic surgeon's knife many times over the decades – including boob jobs, chin tucks and nose jobs – but it is the early vintage models made between 1959 and 1972 that tend to command top prices.

However, take even a vintage Barbie out of her package and she immediately halves in value. Start to play with her and a great potential investment suddenly turns into a fun but largely worthless toy.

GENTLEMEN DON'T PREFER BLONDES

Gentlemen may prefer blondes but Barbie fans will pay more for a red head. Although famous for those platinum blonde locks, the doll occasionally steps out as a brunette, and on even more rare occasions as a flame haired beauty. Investors pay hundreds of pounds more for these unusual hair colours.

Barbie is no bimbo. She is an incredibly independent woman with a fabulous social life and several highly successful careers – ranging from astronaut to sports woman and surgeon – and has the wardrobe to match.

Each year up to 120 new outfits are produced and over the past four decades at least a million different pairs of shoes have been made. Barbie accessories include sports cars, swimming pools, horse stables and more than 40 pets.

Costumes that can make great investments include outfits from modern designers such as Vera Wang, Anna Sui and Terina Tarantino. This clothing can change hands for more than £100 an item.

Vintage Barbie dolls made between 1959 and 1972 are the most collectable but later Mattel-made dolls can still be worth hundreds of pounds. Investors tend to focus on the "Platinum" range of modern Barbie as investments, with their production runs typically having been limited to just a thousand.

LET'S GO PARTY

Guidebooks include *Barbie Doll Field Guide: Values and Identification*, by Dan Stearns. There is no official British Barbie fan club, but a Mattel-backed Barbie Collector club can be found at www.barbiecollector.com. Others include www.ukbarbieclub.co.uk. Check out doll magazine *Haute Doll* for Barbie trading.

Beer

Drinking beer offers a lousy yet pleasurable investment of your time and money. But raise a glass to art, with a limited-edition lager bottle – and you may have an intoxicating winner. Beer can also make you money if you start collecting the beermats on which you rest your foaming pint, the old labels, or related advertising.

German brewery Beck's has been sponsoring Brit Art for the past couple of decades, with different art logo bottles being commissioned most years. As the market for artists' work has soared, so has interest in some of their unique beer-related works.

Tracey Emin was true to her reputation when in 1999 she posed in the bath tastefully sporting "gorgeous breasts" on a beer bottle. With a run of 1500 bottles, an investment costing less than £2 at the off-licence is now worth £1000. A set of four Emin beers sold for £3200 at a charity auction in 2001.

Another highly sought after artist with limited edition prints is cow-pickler Damien Hurst. His dotted renditions were given away in 1995 but can now fetch £500. Others collectables include a "smiley face" bottle by the Chapman brothers, and the Gilbert & George Beck's that launched the concept in 1987.

Sadly, the limited edition art bottles are best consumed visually rather than orally – it is people caving in to the temptation to drink the booze, and not just the love of the art printed on them, that has helped push up their value. Empty bottles are worth far less.

Why not turn your hand to *tegestology* while waiting at the bar? This is the term used for collecting beermats; an art of shrewdness, luck and kleptomania whereby once worthless bits of cardboard can be turned into hundreds of pounds.

The most desired are Watneys beermats from the early Twenties, the first produced in Britain. However, beermat history stretches back to Saxon times, when used to cover beer to stop insects falling into the brew.

Collectable pre-war mats in top condition can fetch anything from £50 to £500. They were made of much thicker cardboard than today. Sought after brewers' mats include Bass, Charrington and Worthington, as well as Mitchell & Butlers.

 ## FLIPPING BEERMATS

Beermat flipping is an art any self-respecting collector must learn as an induction into the world of tegestology. It involves putting a mat half off the table, before bringing your knuckles under the mat and clipping it into the air. The mat must then be caught after completing one revolution, but before it hits the table. Easy? Then try it with more. Another top trick is to skewer beermats using your little finger, with a single focused jab.

Beer bottle labels do not need to be works of art to have collectable value. Some of the older Victorian brewers, whose fabulous brands live on only in the labels, can sell for £100. These include the Dorsetshire Brewery of Sherbourne, which used to quench the thirst with evocative names such as Yeoman Ale and Light Dinner Ale. Other long forgotten but still sought after greats are Wiggins of Stokesley in the North East and Greatorex of Manchester.

Marketing is a separate area for investing, with stout manufacturer Guinness leading the way as one of the greatest of all advertisers. 'Guinness is Good for You' and 'Lovely Day for a Guinness' may no longer pass advertising standards but the famous posters of the Thirties and Forties designed by John Gilroy regularly sell at auction for more than £1000. Later examples, such as 'After Work Guinness' ads from the Sixties, by Tom Eckersley, are still iconic. Top condition examples often change hands for £400.

 ## HERE FOR THE BEER

For more details of beer merchandise trading, festivals and fairs, contact the Campaign for Real Ale, (www.camra.org.uk) or the British Beermat Collectors Society, (www.britishbeermats.org.uk).

The Blues

Woke up this morning feelin' kinda' blue? Then invest in some of those great melancholic tunes. As one of the most influential music genres of the 20th century, the blues is highly collectable.

The blues come from the African-American slaves that worked around the Mississippi delta in the deep south of America. The first authenticated hearing was in 1903 by musician W. C. Handy at a Mississippi railway station.

However, although early music was recorded by jazz singers like Bessie Smith and "Ma" Rainey, it was not until 1925 – when Blind Lemon Jefferson was discovered in Texas by Paramount – that an original blues artist was put on record.

Besides Blind Lemon Jefferson, early musicians such as Charlie Patton, Blind Blake, Son House and Mississippi John Hurt can also be fantastic quality investments. The quality of shellac used for early discs was poor so few good examples of such seminal artists survive. Original printing machines were also destroyed, so the fragile records are the closest anyone can get to their haunting melodies.

A rare Blind Lemon Jefferson disc entitled "Rabbit Foot Blues", which could have been picked up for £2000 a couple of years ago, now might fetch double this amount.

Even in the Twenties and Thirties blues records were relatively expensive, with the early 78s typically costing 75 cents – almost the weekly wage of a labourer. They were cheapest in the Eighties when most vinyl was killed off by CDs.

With titles such as Jefferson's "Match Box Blues", Blake's "Rope Stretching Blues" and Patton's "Mississippi Boll Weevil Blues" you are investing in a painful slice of history and not just a record.

 ## SOLD HIS SOUL TO THE DEVIL

The most popular early bluesman was Robert Johnson, who was reputed to have sold his soul to the devil for miraculously improved guitar-plucking skills. However, the account actually comes from another bluesman Tommy Johnson. To play like the devil he said he sat alone with a guitar by a crossroads at midnight. A mysterious figure allegedly walked up and tuned it so he could play anything.

You can spend even more on ancient blues props than music.

An original Blind Lemon cheap guitar has been valued at £100,000 while find an original photo of Charlie Patton and it could be worth £50,000 as there is only one known to exist.

Sadly, most of the earliest 78s are too valuable and fragile to play. But go for a later wave of blues music from the Forties, Fifties and Sixties, and you can pick up vinyl at bargain prices that will sound far better than a compact disc. The Best Of Muddy Waters first-pressing recorded in 1957 is a great starting point and can be picked up for £50. Other collectables include Howling Wolf, Sonny Boy Williamson II, Elmore James, Jimmy Reed and John Lee Hooker.

An indication of their potential investment value is the price of albums from early rock groups who they inspired. A Rolling Stones Now album from 1964, snapped up for £20 just over a decade ago, might now sell for £400.

GETTING THE BLUES

Second-hand shops are a great place to start for advice. Good books include *Deep Blues* by Robert Palmer and *The Penguin Guide to Blues Recordings* by Tony Russell and Chris Smith. See also the magazine *Blues Matters*, www.bluesmatters.com.

Bonsai Trees

Money may not grow on trees but green-fingered investors can still nurture a tidy profit through the ancient art of growing a bonsai. Those with the right skills – and plenty of patience – can transform a £50 sapling investment into a mature miniature tree worth more than £1000 within a couple of decades.

Bonsais are not dwarf species but are trees that have been forced to stay small. This is done by rigorously pruning and shaping roots with artistic skill, so that the tree appears naturally strong and weatherworn, but in Lilliputian proportions.

Although you could start with just the price of a seed, the most practical solution is to visit a specialist garden nursery or a bonsai centre. Sapling prices start at about £5, though enthusiasts often fork out £200 for a starter tree.

The most popular tree choices are maples, pines, junipers and elms, with prices varying depending on age, species and quality of sapling.

A key mistake made by first-time bonsai growers is purchasing an indoor plant, as it is used to tropical climates and could die within a couple of months. Opt for an outdoor version, which can be kept in a tray or pot on a pedestal, and only bring it indoors during particularly harsh winter conditions.

The pot is an intrinsic part of the bonsai experience, as well as a stand to show off the prized possession. Specialist pruning gear may also be useful, while patience, dedication and skill are other necessary ingredients.

MADE IN JAPAN

The word *bonsai* is Japanese for "shallow tray plant", and is the art of capturing the essence of the natural world in miniature. The ancient art began in China more than 2000 years ago – known there as Penjing – and was picked up by the Japanese in the 11th century. The most valuable trees in the world are worth at least £1m and meticulously looked after within the Imperial Collection in Japan. They are also among the oldest, with some more than 700 years old.

The secret of bonsai success is for the gardener to treat the tree as a living sculpture, with the miniature tree being skilfully crafted rather than just grown. The bonsai should have a realistically weathered and untameable look.

The tree must look well proportioned and in harmony with its surroundings. To achieve this level of success, a bonsai may require almost daily pampering, with several hours spent on delicate grooming on occasion.

Ham-fisted novices would be well advised to pay an expert to tender their mini-garden and learn from this experience, taking note of the delicate nature of professional grooming. A bonsai master may charge £300 for a full cut.

Auctions are few and far between, and most sales are done via word of mouth within the tight-knit bonsai-growing community of clubs and specialist traders.

Novices should pick up one of the many bonsai books for initial buying tips and growing advice. They should also seek out their local bonsai clubs for practical help through the Federation of British Bonsai Societies.

GROWING AN INTEREST

The Federation of British Bonsai Societies website: www.fobbsbonsai.co.uk; Friends of The National Collection, Birmingham Botanical Gardens (www.nationalbonsaicollection.org).

Bubble Cars

The bubble car came from the British Allied victory over Germany in World War II. Aircraft makers Messerschmitt and Henkel, along with BMW, were banned from making planes that might pose a threat to European peace. Forced to turn their minds to other matters, their skilful engineers came up with the micro car for the cash-strapped nation.

The cars' fortunes rose from fuel hikes caused by the 1956 Suez Crisis, but the decline came soon after with the arrival of the 1959 Austin Mini – though a few three-wheelers limped on. For many years they were ridiculed as figures of fun but in the past two decades they have become rare and valuable investments.

The Messerschmitt KR175 rolled off the production line in 1953 with a transparent acrylic bubble canopy that earned the vehicles their nickname. It was followed up with a modified KR200 two years later that ran on a 173cc two-stroke engine with a 50mph top speed.

Then came the comparatively racy TG500 – a four-wheeler "Tiger" – which could overtake the competition at a respectable 65mph. Only about 60 Tigers still exist and they can now sell for up to £30,000: shooting up a third in value since 2000.

The same Tiger might have changed hands for less than £100 in the Seventies.

Other European bubble car makers include Isetta, manufactured under license by BMW, Vespa, and Henkel. The French also made "voiturettes". All these manufacturers' vehicles now regularly change hands for thousands of pounds.

ONLY FOOLS AND HORSES

The most famous three-wheeler of all is the yellow Reliant driven by the Trotter siblings in the BBC TV comedy series *Only Fools and Horses*. One of the TV prop cars was bought for £44,000 in 2007 by boxer Ricky Hatton. The vehicle was a Reliant Robin derivation known as the Reliant Regal Supervan.

Three wheels were often better than four in the bubble car heyday in Britain, as it often enabled them to avoid the steeper four-wheeler road tax.

The Bond Bug was an English three-wheel two-seater built by Reliant between 1970 and 1974 and coloured tangerine orange. It compared favourably with four-wheelers of the era, managing 78mph on a 700cc engine. New it cost £629, and now sells for at least £4000.

Other British bubble car collectables include Berkeleys and the Meadows Frisky.

JEDI KNIGHT RIDER

Jedi Knight Luke Skywalker used a Bond Bug in the sci-fi movie *Star Wars* as his chosen mode of planetary transport. The Bond chassis was used for the Landspeeder he drove on his home world of Tatooine. The wheels were hidden by car mirrors, attached to the vehicle body, which pointed 45 degrees to the ground.

Bubble car investors will only find it a satisfying bet if they can accept unreliable performance, expensive maintenance and discomfort as part of the thrill. Join an enthusiasts club for advice and make sure you take an expert to check out any vehicles. After purchase it will need regular care and attention – ideally living in a garage – to keep or grow in value.

CHASE UP

The Bubble Car Museum in Cranwell, Lincolnshire, offers a fun introduction to the bubble car. It also has details of the huge number of specialist bubble car clubs in Britain (www.bubblecarmuseum.co.uk). Clubs include the Messerschmitt Owners' Club at www.messerschmitt.co.uk.

Butterflies

The Queen Alexandra's Birdwing is the largest butterfly in the world. Fluttering about in a remote corner of Papua New Guinea it boasts a dazzling coat of greens, blues and gold, on a wingspan that can measure more than a foot across.

Early adventurers were so desperate to hunt down this elusive bird-like butterfly that they sometimes resorted to blasting it out of the sky with a shotgun – thereby capturing little more than the tatty remnants of an insect. This helps explain why so few of these extremely rare and exotic butterflies were ever caught in one piece, and how their value has soared to as much as £20,000 each.

Hunt one illegally and you are liable to go to jail.

The Queen Alexandra's Birdwing is not the only exotic butterfly that changes hands for lots of money. Others include the ferocious looking tiger-eyed Bhutanitis lidderdalii of Bhutan and a green orchid-like Ornithoptera chimaera.

A private collection of 3500 beautiful swallowtail butterflies, collected by the eccentric explorer Charles Rothschild between 1899 and his death in 1937, was sold for more than £80,000 by Harrow school in 2009.

Less expensive collectables include the bright metallic blue Morpho didius, available for as little as £25 and Calodema butterflies, such as the Regale Blairi and Regale, which can cost up to £300.

VLADIMIR NABOKOV

Author Vladimir Nabokov was an avid butterfly collector. He was the leading lepidopterist on the American family of "blue" Polyommatinae. He wrote extensively on the subject – in addition to his bestsellers like *Lolita*. The famous author died in 1977, after a fall in the Alps when out butterfly-hunting.

A typical Victorian hunter would dash around the countryside with a giant net and keep a deadly array of killing bottles and setting boards at home for the butterflies.

These days lepidopterists – the term for butterfly collectors – still enjoy one of the most gentle of field sports, but capture butterflies for breeding rather than killing and displaying them. A female butterfly can typically lay more than 200 eggs, and if well looked after in controlled conditions they can all be reared into adulthood.

There are at least 20,000 different butterfly species across the world of which only 59 live in Britain. The numbers are dwindling due to a loss of natural habitat and recent wet summers. Among those on the danger list are the High Brown Fritillary, Pearl-bordered Fritillary and Wood White. The largest and most rare butterfly in Britain is the British Swallowtail, found only in Norfolk fenland where it lives off parsley.

BUTTERFLY ART

The most valuable butterflies are those collections stuck on canvas by "artist" Damien Hurst. Footballer David Beckham is believed to have splashed out £250,000 for a montage of wings in 2003, while a couple of 7ft square butterfly assortments entitled "The Agony and the Ecstasy" sold for $1.3m in 2003.

Papua New Guinea has a thriving industry where villagers are encouraged to boost the population of butterflies by being paid to grow plants on which they lay eggs. There are also sustainable butterfly farms in Thailand and Malaysia.

Butterflies on display need to be stored away from direct sunlight as otherwise their brightly coloured wings will fade. They can also be susceptible to being eaten by certain beetle larvae.

 ENJOY A FLUTTER

The butterfly pleasure these days is all about helping the endangered species survive, something which can be combined naturally with an interest in investing and trading in preserved specimens. See Butterfly Conservation at www.butterfly-conservation.org. Useful books for investors include *The Aurelian Legacy: British Butterflies and their Collectors*, by Michael Salmon.

Cameras

Despite the digital revolution, demand for the best film-based camera models is still very much alive. However, only a few are worth snapping up as potential investments, so adventurous investors should enter the market with due caution.

Leica is the top investment model and takes snaps superior to most cameras today. Twenty years ago, collectors could buy a 1954 Leica Rangefinder M3 for £250 – and a decade later it was worth £1000.

Then the film market collapsed with the arrival of digital cameras. After falling steeply, values eventually recovered to £600. Yet if still in its original box, the Leica can command a price of £2000.

German engineering is most in demand, with coveted names other than Leica including Zeiss Contax and Voigtländer. Of these a top collectable is early Fifties Voigtländer BESSA II, with stunning Apo-Lanthar lens – fetching up to £2000. The German Rolleiflex range of cameras also holds market values well. Twin-lens Rolleiflex 3.5F examples from the early Sixties – as used by photographer David Bailey – now cost £500, but still offer fabulous picture quality.

A top British pedigree is the former aircraft instrument maker Reid and Sigrist, while another home grown skilled manufacturer is Corfield. A modern super-wide angle Corfield WA67 model can cost £2200.

After World War II, the Japanese borrowed German camera engineering know-how and in some cases improved on it through their own companies – which included Nikon, Canon and Pentax. The post-war Nikon Rangefinders are particularly collectable – they still offer great pictures but are not part of the SLR camera range. Classics include the 1957 Nikon SP, which has a market value for a top example of about £1600.

Modern models can also fetch top prices. In 1994, Leitz Camera Company made 100 Leica M6s to mark the centenary of the Royal Photographic Society. With matching 50mm-ft Summicron lens, it costs £4000.

SPY CAMERA

The Swiss Tessina miniature camera was often used by spies during the Cold War and fitted 35mm film in special cassettes. Examples from the early Sixties can be found for £350. Cameras disguised as cigarette lighters from the Fifties can be £2000. A Krauss Photo-Revolver is £4000, while a discreet powder contact and lipstick camera costs £1000. Secret agents snapped by an 1890 French-made Bloch Photo-Cravate, hidden in the tie, were caught on camera by a device now worth up to £15,000.

Frenchman Louis-Jacques Daguerre took the world's first photograph on January 2nd 1839. It was a photo of the moon and at the time artists feared the end of painting. It wasn't until 1900 that Eastman Dry Plate & Film Company of America began mass-producing the Kodak Brownie, which can still be snapped up for just a few pounds.

Wet-plate cameras from the 1860s can be picked up for £1200. These were typically wooden boxes without manufacturers details or shutter. A cap was put over the lens after a 30-second exposure, with the cameraman hidden under a cloak.

British Victorian collectables include the late 19th century Sanderson, with red folding concertina bellows, which can be picked up for £300. Another historic curiosity is an early Twenties Ensign camera of mahogany, teak and brass.

 ZOOM IN ON A CAMERA INVESTMENT

Invest £25 to join the Photographic Collectors' Club of Britain for guidance, local help, and information on fairs and specialist traders. Visit their website at www.pccgb.com. Industry must-read *McKeown's Price Guide to Antique and Classic Cameras* has information on more than 40,000 different models.

Camper Vans

T he spirit of adventure still lives on for those who invest in a Volkswagen Bus — they can travel the world in camper van-style, while the wheels beneath their feet keep rising in value.

The top money goes on the iconic Type 2 model "splitty", with its divided windscreen, which was made between 1949 and 1967. Some models have more than doubled in value over the past 15 years.

The Samba is the most sought after variation, with 23 windows and eight skylights. The Deluxe Micro Bus from 1950-1967 can sell for £25,000 if in polished chrome condition. A decade ago the same vehicle could have been purchased for £15,000 in great condition, or £8000 if in need of loving care.

But the most valuable camper investment that gets enthusiasts drooling is the ultra rare pre-1955 "barn door" model without front air-scoops, which fetches up to £40,000.

The later VW "bay window" Type 2 camper van, made between 1967 and 1979, has also captured the imagination of flower power investors, and is far more affordable. A great "bay window" can cost £10,000, while even a tatty model in need of restoration is hard to find under £5000. A decade ago a bus was half the price.

The "wedge" Type 25, made between 1979 and 1992, is also enjoying an increased following, with investors typically having to part with at least £4000 to join in the outdoors motoring fun.

MEIN KAMPFER VAN

Adolf Hitler has a key role to play in the development of the Volkswagon Bus. It was wheeled off the production line in 1949 as a direct descendant of the "Strength Through Joy Car" VW Beatle, unveiled by the Fuhrer in 1938.

As an investment, keep vehicles in as original condition as possible. At least two-thirds of all splitty campers have had their suspension lowered, and many have regrettably been "pimped" with alloy wheels.

Volkswagen did not manufacture motor homes but allowed other firms to install cookers, beds and other camping set-ups in its buses under license – an expert can help check on authenticity. The best are generally recognised to be the German caravan maker Westfalia, known as the "Westy". Other great conversions came from Torquay-based "Devon", the Folkstone-based "Dormobile" and the Sidmouth-based "Danbury".

They may look the most cool, but the early buses were not designed for speed – and with a 1500cc engine they puff along motorways at little more than 60 mph.

In 1970, a 1.7 litre engine was fitted; and in 1973, front indicators were moved from below to above the headlamps. The 1.8 litre arrived in 1974, while in 1976 2.0 litre engines were installed, allowing healthier top speeds of 80mph.

SOURCE: JOHN HAYES
HTTP://WWW.MOTORNSTUFFART.CO.UK

If you want to make money out of a camper van then the best way to save on mechanics' bills is to do any necessary work yourself – otherwise find someone good that you can trust.

LIVING THE DREAM

Before embarking on the surfer dude dream, join a club to learn about what is on the market, visiting VW meetings and fairs, and find experts who can help out. Clubs include the Split Screen Van Club (www.ssvc.org.uk); VW Type 2 Owners Club (www.vwt2oc.com); and www.club80-90.co.uk, which focuses on "wedge'" models. A useful trading website is www.thesamba.com.

Celebrity Hair

The value of famous hair has soared five-fold over the past decade thanks to a new breed of investors desperate for follicles of historical interest. Icons such as Lord Nelson, whose locks could be picked up for £500 a decade ago, now have investors' hair standing on end at prices up to £20,000.

Even a few strands from a star's bonce – such as a tiny snip of an Elvis Presley quiff – costing about £100 ten years ago, will now fetch at least £300. And a three-inch mass of dark cuttings from "The King" fetched £72,791 in 2002.

The biggest bargain finds often require a certain amount of ingenuity. Astronaut Neil Armstrong was far from over the moon when his barber sold a lock of his hair for £1600 a few years ago.

Unfortunately, the investment potential from the average head of hair is usually limited to what a wig manufacturer may offer for it – about £40 for a full set of lengthy locks.

 ## LINCOLN'S BAD HAIR DAY

John Reznikoff, president of the University Archives at the University of Connecticut, Stamford, US, has the world's largest collection of celebrity hair. With more than 115 famous hair snippets, from Marilyn Monroe to Napoleon, he even owns a piece of President Lincoln's hair – from when it was cut to allow doctors to get a look at the assassination bullet hole. (This is worth an astonishing £650,000.) He also possesses the only known example of Einstein DNA, in a few strands of hair worth £10,000.

Just like autographs and other personal memorabilia, hair has collectable cachet, but value has only really exploded in recent years. A key attraction is that hair samples contain DNA, which provides a scientific blueprint of the original owner. However, making sure the hair is the real thing is not easy and does require a certain leap of faith. Always demand authentic documents of proof, and if possible see if it has been scientifically tested.

Celebrity hair wigs are also collectable. A Hollywood actress hairpiece belonging to Halle Berry in one of the *X-Men* movies sold for £4000, while flamboyant head-warmers from Elton John have been known to go for £5000. As a rule of thumb, stick to safer celebrities, like Joan Collins and Tina Turner, who do not hide what they use. Examples by more reticent stars, such as Paul Daniels, will be harder to find, as vanity keeps them off the market.

A specialist dealer, as said, will typically only offer up to £40 for a full head of long hair. At an average of £3 an ounce for hair more than six inches long, or £5 an ounce if over 12 inches, it is a time consuming way to make extra cash. The average hair only grows between 0.3mm and 0.5mm a day.

It is, therefore, rather a poor way to make money in the modern era – although sales from sponsored charity hair shaves provide a novel idea for making a few pounds for good causes.

In either case, the hair is put to good use, and turned into wigs costing £1000 or more.

A REAL SNIP

Rooting out investment hair requires cunning and guile. Befriend a celebrity barber or simply ask a star for a small lock. Celebrity wigs are occasionally sold at specialist movie and theatrical auctions.

Chess

The first recorded reference to the oldest game of skill in the world comes in the 6th century, when it was introduced to Persia from India – though its origins may date as far back as 2500 BC.

Chess came to Britain at the end of the 11th century, from the First Crusade. However, some of the rules and pieces from that time would be hard to interpret for modern day players. It wasn't until the release of the Staunton chess set in 1849 that a universally recognised game was born.

Collectable chess sets that were selling for £300 or £400 in the Eighties are now going for about £1500, while the rarest pieces continue to hold their value thanks to growing appreciation of their historic appeal. Not surprisingly, the most ancient sets are the most valuable. The top price paid is £828,750 in 2000 for a single ivory king, thought to have been made in Egypt or Syria for a 10th century Muslim chess set. It had been purchased the previous year by an eagle-eyed auction hunter for just £1000.

John Company ivory chess sets of the 18th and 19th century, commissioned by the East India Company, are also highly sought after, as they were so beautifully made. Often depicting Indians fighting the British, the sets can fetch £20,000 or more – a couple of decades ago they were changing hands for about £5000.

Early Staunton chess sets are very popular and still playable. They were named after then chess world champion Howard Staunton and made by the croquet game maker John Jacques of London. Early 19th century Staunton sets may fetch £300 or £1000-£2000 if particularly well made and in original boxes.

THE GRANDEST OF GRAND MASTERS

The greatest of all time? Possibly Garry Kasparov, who narrowly – sometimes controversially – took the crown and held it from fellow Russian all-time great Anatoly Karpov throughout the Eighties and Nineties. Another contender is American-born Bobby Fischer, who forfeited his crown to Karpov after failing to turn up.

A chess set should be judged by its pawns. A master carver focused on the King and Queen, with Knight, Bishop and Rook tackled by experienced craftsmen. Pawns were often polished off by apprentices. If you come across a superbly made pawn it indicates that the master carver completed the whole set.

Handle before buying. Sets with missing pieces are worth far less, so forgeries are common. A fake is likely to feel sharper to the touch than rounded pieces that have been handled through many years of playing. Individual ivory forgeries can look bleached and not as shiny as the other pieces.

Collectable chess sets can be made of a huge range of materials, including ivory, bone, porcelain, precious metals, glass and wood. Figures are even more varied, but among the most sought after are those with historic themes and figures, such as from the Napoleonic Wars.

Rooks come in all shapes and sizes – including camels and elephants. The name derives from the Arabic *rukh*, meaning camel-mounted soldier. On some Indian sets, a turreted "castle" charged across the board on the back of an elephant.

FINDING A CHECK MATE

Don't collect if you can't play. Many grew up with classic starter *Chess for Children*, by Raymond Bott and Stanley Morrison; other guides include *Chessmen* by Frank Greygoose. Visit Chess Collectors International at www.chesscollectors.com.

Christmas Cards

T he true spirit of Christmas is certainly found in the cards handed out in Victorian and Edwardian Britain, long before the celebration was grimly hijacked by the crasser commercialism of our age.

Thanks to the introduction of a chromolithographic process from around 1860, many Christmas cards were packed with vibrant colours, often of superior vividness to those used today. The Victorians were also highly inventive, with plenty of novelty designs offering different shapes, pop-ups, and even mechanical and bird "squeaker" cards.

Exchanging Christmas cards was an expensive pursuit only afforded by the wealthy. The cards were so highly prized that Victorians would often put them in special albums – they would typically exchange no more than a dozen a year.

Many that were seen as almost worthless novelty items just a few years ago can now change hands as a fascinating investment worth tens or hundreds of pounds.

A key appeal of the cards is that they provide a unique piece of social history that embodies firsthand the Victorian lifestyle, humour, religiosity, and abiding love of nature and festivity.

In 1843, the first 1000 hand-coloured cards, showing a family toasting the season, were commissioned by Sir Henry Cole (future director of the Victoria and Albert Museum).

At the time these J.C. Horsley-illustrated cards sold for the princely sum of a shilling. Only about nine of these cards have survived, and can sell for as much as £8469 each at auction. A decade ago the same card cost £2000.

The heyday of the Christmas card was the 1880s, when it also started to capture the imagination of the middle classes – though it was still a luxury item. These had verse inside and often used comic animals, such as dressed up pets and monkeys, or traditional snow scenes depicting nature or sports like hunting and skating. Charles Dickens' seasonal images were also popular.

Early card publishers that are among the most collectable include Raphael Tuck & Sons, De La Rue and Marcus Ward & Co.

THE REAL FATHER CHRISTMAS

The real St Nicholas was a 4th century Turkish bishop and Father Christmas derives from a German translation of him as Kris Kringle. The Dutch translation Sinterklaas turned him into Santa Claus. St Nicholas climbed roofs and dropped purses down chimneys, which landed in girls' stockings.

Modern merchandisers hi-jacked the saintly Christian figure to cash in on the season of goodwill by promoting their own goods. Santa became jolly, rosy-cheeked and rotund after advertisers for Coca-Cola adopted him in the Thirties.

The Christmas tree was introduced by Prince Albert in 1841 and appeared on cards within a few years. Holly appeared in 1848, while robins did not grace a card until the 1850s. After 1870 Christmas cards could be sent in an unsealed envelope for a ha'penny and Father Christmas began to be used.

By the early Edwardian era, Santa Claus themed cards were commonplace – though he was still St Nicholas. He not only wore red tunics, but also purple, green, blue and white. The more unusual colours tend to fetch the most.

Among the most sought after cards of the Edwardian era are hold-to-light Santa cards worth as much as £100 each today – a decade ago they could be picked up for less than £20.

Although there are plenty of great modern Christmas cards with original and eye-catching designs they fail to attract investor attention, as the vast majority are mass-produced.

INVESTMAS

Anyone interested in collecting Christmas cards might like to start with the Ephemera Society at www.ephemera-society.org.uk. A good place to meet traders and collectors is at an Ephemera Society fair.

Cigarette Cards

Back in the good old days cigarettes were cool, manly and a symbol of outdoor fun and adventure. Occasionally, they also gave you cancer. To promote the positive side, and push brand awareness, cigarette cards were introduced.

It began as a stiffener to stop paper packets of cigarettes getting squashed. But by the late 1880s marketing messages were being included, and by 1895 general interest sets were being introduced. Lots of Victorian themes swiftly followed that appealed to gentlemen of the era (and those remaining in spirit today) – with an abundance of patriotic military pictures, depictions of sports like football, cricket and horse racing, as well as stylish images of royalty, historic figures and actresses.

Cards were typically designed in sets of 50 and full sets from the 1890s are among the most valuable. An 1899 set of theatre actresses might go under the hammer for £700, while 1896 cricketers can fetch £3000.

Cigarette cards continued to grow in popularity, with thousands issued in the early 20th century. Later sets tend to be cheaper as more have survived, but still provide fascination as collectables that can at the very least hold their value and their charm. Sets from the Twenties, such as Flags of the British Empire or Household Hints, can still be picked up for £20.

However, with the outbreak of World War II paper rationing hit the industry hard and the market never fully recovered.

The most collectable British maker for cartophilists – card collectors – is James Taddy. Founded in 1740 as a purveyor of tea, snuff and tobacco, the company was renowned for the quality of its Edwardian cards.

However, in 1920 striking workers received the ultimatum: 'Return to work or I close the factory.' Owner Gilliat Hatfield was a man of his word and, when the union directed the workers to defy this, the factory duly closed. Taddy brands Myrtle Grove and Premier vanished overnight – forever.

So also did the cigarette cards Taddy's Clowns. A set of 20 of these cards can change hands for £15,000 today – in the Seventies the same set fetched £1000.

TOBACCO TABOO

The record price paid for a cigarette card is $2.8m – about £1.5m – paid in 2007 for one displaying an early 20th century American baseball star called Honus Wagner. The sportsman was an anti-smoker and refused to feature on any cigarette cards – even going to court to stop the production of any with him on. However, this one somehow managed to sneak out.

Condition is everything for the cigarette card collector and a pristine example worth several pounds suddenly becomes worthless if in fairly tatty condition.

Sets put into scrap books plunge in value because the pictures are usually accompanied by words and collector details on the back of the cards.

However, stumble across a card with an error or misprint and you may have a unique investment that is worth hundreds rather than just a few pence. Examples spotted in the past include a Player's picture of a 22-year-old Benjamin Disraeli in 1826 standing in front of Big Ben before it was even built.

Another can be found in a series of Famous Escapes for Turf cigarettes, where one card showed Napoleon III escaping the Prussians with words referring to Winston Churchill.

CARD TRADING

The London Cigarette Card Company is a trader and publishes the definitive industry price guide *The Cigarette Card Catalogue*, priced £7 (www.londoncigcard.co.uk). Other card traders include Murray Cards (www.murraycards.com) and www.cigarettecards.co.uk.

Classic Cars

Buying a classic car may not be the best route to a fast fortune but can be one of the most fun investments you will ever make. A wisely purchased old motor will hold its value if well looked after, and climb steadily in price over the years.

As a bonus, it also offers an excuse to enjoy the open road in style and take pleasure in an exciting vintage vehicle that turns heads wherever you go. Compared to this, a modern vehicle depreciates the moment it is driven off the garage forecourt, and can fall in price by as much as half within just a year.

The process of finding out which car you might like to buy should be a pleasurable pursuit and there are plenty of books in libraries and bookshops to spark the imagination.

As a rule of thumb, spend the maximum you can afford. Even if you plan to do much of the mechanical work yourself, the state of the vehicle is key – so seek out the very best.

Motorists on a tight budget might consider a well looked after Triumph Herald convertible for £4000, a Morris Minor Traveller at £7000, MGB Roadster at £8000 and similarly priced Sixties Mini Cooper – or even a £5000 Ford Capri.

Those with deeper pockets can step back into the Sixties heyday for a pristine condition E-type Jaguar for £35,000, an Austin Healey 3000 for £28,000, or opt for a well-kept mid-Fifties Lotus Six costing £20,000.

Other great classics include vintage Volvo, Fiat, BMW or Mercedes Benz vehicles, while sturdy old Land Rovers are renowned for holding values well.

 ## SCREWDRIVER TEST

Try to ignore the smooth sales patter but prod away with a screwdriver in search of nasty surprises. This involves taking a good look underneath and giving it a thorough test drive. Ask to see the paperwork and details of previous owners. Careful owners will have kept all the bills and receipts – always a good sign.

There is no definitive guide on what makes a classic car, although those registered before 1973 escape road tax because of their age. Not surprisingly, old vehicles are the most rare and often the most valuable if still in good condition. But an important consideration for modern motorists isn't just the sexy curves of the motor but also the comfort for our pampered 21st century behinds. Heating systems were not introduced into most vehicles until the Sixties and seating was often relatively uncomfortable. It is also worth remembering fuel consumptions of early vehicles can be high and they do not run on unleaded fuel.

A garage is ideal for older vehicles but if the vehicle is well looked-after and regularly serviced then there is no reason why it cannot live on the side of the street.

On the downside, a classic motor cannot be trusted to complete a journey without ever having a problem. It is important to regularly service old vehicles and budget for nasty surprises.

JOIN THE CLUB

The best place to start is a local motoring owners' club, of which there are hundreds across the country, for advice and a guide on prices and what is for sale. When checking a vehicle, visit with an expert or friend if possible, making sure to look below the surface sheen and shiny chrome. Look out for knocking noises from the engine, corroded chassis, ill-fitting doors and filler hiding rust.

A full breakdown of different car clubs is available on a link at the website www.classic-car-directory.com and details can also be found in specialist classic car magazines, such as *Practical Classics* and *Classic & Sports Car*.

Cocktail Shakers

What ho! When the sun sinks below the yardarm – a mast spur that holds up your sail – the afternoon cocktail hour has arrived. Lounge lizards and flappers can relax with a sharpener, enjoyed in authentic period style with a real shaker.

The contraption is typically just a cylinder with strainer and cap. The function is simple – combine ingredients of a drink, chill with ice, and strain so the ice stays behind and doesn't dilute the cocktail. The tricky bit is the skill required in ensuring the recipe for success is just right.

The mixers used for providing such fabulous concoctions as the Martini, Margarita and Manhattan began life in the 19th century as a contraption that resembled a coffee pot. The first design patent was granted to New Yorker William Harnett in 1872. But it was prohibition in 1920 that turned the cocktail hour into an American institution. Bars closed and the secret drinking dens of the speakeasy were born. Bootleg booze was mixed with cocktail ingredients to hide poor quality alcohol.

The shakers from the Twenties and Thirties really capture investors' imagination, a time when luxury brands such as Asprey, Cartier and Tiffany began churning out cocktail accessories. These now go for thousands of pounds. An Asprey Thirst Extinguisher cocktail shaker costing seven guineas in 1932 might presently rattle investors for £2000. Meanwhile a classic art deco Manhattan shaker designed by Norman Bel Geddes won't see any change remain from £1000.

However, for those who want some money left over to buy the cocktail ingredients, post-war stylish shakers from the Fifties and Sixties can still provide suavity and value for money – for less than £100.

  STIRRED NOT SHAKEN

The art of creating the perfect dry Martini can take years to learn. Ice-cold gin, sparing use of vermouth, plus olives – or a twist of lemon. However, to shake is a crime according to many mixologists, as this "bruises" the alcohol and froths the drink. James Bond chooses to shake merely so as to achieve an instantly chilled drink. And, for an extra dry Martini, follow the instructions of Winston Churchill. He suggested pouring gin into a pitcher while glancing briefly at a bottle of vermouth across the room.

Aesthetic appeal is key. If you think a shaker looks sleek and sexy, others will too. Close your eyes and imagine how silver screen cocktail fans like Marlene Dietrich, Joan Crawford or Humphrey Bogart might view your equipment.

Shakers come in all shapes and sizes – the bullet-shaped options being one of the most appealing. Other sought after designs include zeppelins, skyscrapers, lighthouses, penguins and rockets. Single drink mixers may look cute but are far less practical. Themes such as golf will also add to investment attraction.

Silver and glass are the favoured materials among connoisseurs – often silver and chrome plated – but there are also plenty of great designs in Bakelite, plastic, aluminium, stainless steel and porcelain.

Bumps and scratches can often be fixed by an expert, but the problem of missing pieces from a set are not so easy to mend: complete sets of mixers and glasses are the most valuable.

 ## JOINING THE COCKTAIL SET

Whet the appetite with out-of-print read, *The Cocktail Shaker* by Simon Khachadovrian. Thorough research will also be necessary, with the requisite commitment and stamina to cope with hangovers. Rummage through flea markets for bargains. Vintage cocktail shakers also turn up at antique markets and auctions.

Comics

Anyone who thinks cartoon strips are just for kids might grow up fast when they discover that the most valuable comics can sell for as much as £600,000 – the modern-day price of a pristine 1938 issue of *Action*, in which Superman first appeared. That's not a bad return for an initial pocket money investment of ten cents.

And Batman is not far behind. The first sighting of the caped crusader, in the 27th issue of *Detective Comics* in 1939, is now worth as much as £485,000. A decade ago the same issue was changing hands for less than £100,000. Even a near-mint 1962 copy of *Amazing Fantasy* 15, when spectacle-wearing Peter Parker got bitten by a spider to become Spider-Man, can set you back £30,000.

Other superhero greats include the Fantastic Four, launched with their own comic strip in 1961, the Avengers and X-Men, both launched in 1963, and Captain America, who joined Allied Forces in the fight against Hitler in 1941.

 ## UNDERPANTS MAN

Contrary to popular belief, Superman does not wear his underpants on the outside. That fetching pair of red briefs is actually a support outfit as used by circus strongmen – there is a belt clearly visible on the top of the stretchy shorts. The safety truss should help the superhero avoid suffering a hernia.

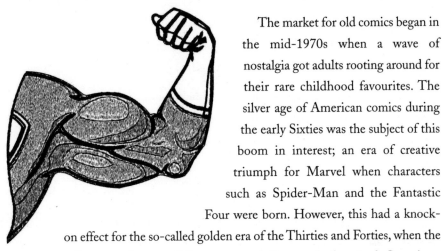

The market for old comics began in the mid-1970s when a wave of nostalgia got adults rooting around for their rare childhood favourites. The silver age of American comics during the early Sixties was the subject of this boom in interest; an era of creative triumph for Marvel when characters such as Spider-Man and the Fantastic Four were born. However, this had a knock-on effect for the so-called golden era of the Thirties and Forties, when the very first superheroes of Superman and Batman had arrived. Superhero movies have also fuelled the market.

Thanks to parents spring cleaning their children's bedrooms and treating piles of comics as rubbish, very few copies of these early American cartoon strips survive – which has sent values rocketing.

Bargain hunters may want to look out for current comics but must be wary that so-called limited editions will probably not be that rare. It is storylines, illustrators and fads that may eventually turn into valuable investments for comic lovers. Popular recent successes include a first issue of *Ultimate Spider-Man*, issued in 2000, which soon cleared the shelves thanks to a very successful modernised Peter Parker storyline. It can now fetch £100.

Condition is key in the comics market and copies are graded accordingly. Near-mint (nm) is like brand new, and the most sought after quality for investors. Well-thumbed but unharmed comics are worth half this price: very good (vg) to fine (fn). Tears or marks can slash values to a tenth of the top price and will usually be graded as fair (fr).

Collectors rarely touch anything less than fine. Investors should always buy the best quality they can afford, as the state of the comic is of primary concern to any collector; as are all possible original extras, such as free gifts.

Although they may look good on the bookshelf, comics should be kept in a dry place, in acid-free bags, out of direct sunlight – which causes them to yellow – and far away from the children for whom they were intended.

JOINING THE CAPED CRUSADERS

One of the best places to start is *Comics International,* an enthusiasts' magazine available at comic shops. It lists specialist traders and comic marts, where buyers and sellers meet for deals. Industry bible *Overstreet Comic Book Price Guide* offers full listings but prices tend to be dated.

Competition Entry

Question: Can you explain in no more than three words how to win lots of money?
Answer: By entering competitions.

"Compers" are people who have turned competitions into a moneymaking art. Using dedication and skill they can travel the world, win luxuries such as cars, pay off their mortgage, and earn a healthy income – all by diligently filling in forms.

However, you must make your own luck in the world of competitions. This means the most successful compers knuckle down to complete at least 25 brainteasers a day. Whether found on the back of a tin of baked beans, as the monthly prize draw in a glossy magazine, or by tuning into a radio show, the prevalence of opportunities means that any spare moment requires a pen to be poised in hand.

The secret of winning is to enter as many competitions as possible to improve the odds. This means cruising the supermarket aisles in search of competitions and getting tips from friends, as well as subscribing to specialist competition magazines that list hundreds of prizes up for grabs each month.

Be prepared for a huge range of prizes – from a pound of sausages to a world cruise. But it is important to enter for as many competitions as possible, regardless of how interesting, as practice is key if you want to succeed. (If you look after the pounds of pork, the piña coladas on the Pacific will look after themselves.)

Tips for improving your chances include checking the small print of prize draws to see if you can make multiple entries. By posting in answers at different times you can also boost the jackpot odds. For local lucky dips, coloured envelopes and eye-catching postcards also improve your chances. Searching out obscure competitions is also a good bet, as they may attract just a handful of entrants.

BEANZ MEANZ WINZ

The comper looking to make the most of their skills should look no further than the legendary baked beans slogan, which was actually provided by a competition winner: "Beanz Meanz Heinz". This is the kind of original catchy phrase that may guide you to success. Alliterations, humour, sound-bite words, double-meanings and rhyme all help when providing sentences for similar competitions.

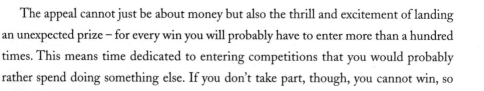

The appeal cannot just be about money but also the thrill and excitement of landing an unexpected prize – for every win you will probably have to enter more than a hundred times. This means time dedicated to entering competitions that you would probably rather spend doing something else. If you don't take part, though, you cannot win, so not being in the mood is no excuse for a hardened comper.

Apart from the time needed to be set aside there is also the hefty postage bill. And it is best altogether to avoid all rip-off "premium rate" phone competitions – you are likely to end up a loser.

Plenty of the competition gifts will not have a cash alternative offered as a prize. A key part of the skill of being a successful comper is therefore knowing how to dispose of the unwanted prizes. This is typically done by advertising in the local press or selling winnings to neighbours and friends. Another popular marketplace for this kind of thing is of course eBay.

DISCOVER A WINNING FORMULA

Luck has little to do with it – hard graft by entering as many competitions as possible is what really swings the odds in your favour. Start by subscribing to dedicated comper publications to get a full list of what is on the market, plus a few useful tips. Also keep an eye out for local competitions where odds of winning tend to be higher.

Publications include *Competitor's Companion* (see the website www.accoladepublishing.co.uk). Other website links to comper magazines include www.compersnews.co.uk and www.theprizefinder.com.

Corkscrews

The first cork stoppers to keep an airtight seal, allowing wine to be easily transported and stored for years, were introduced in the early 17th century – giving immediate rise to demand for the invention of the corkscrew.

The earliest examples were simple designs based on a screw-shaped "worm" used by gunsmiths to clean a gun barrel of debris and trapped shot. Although rudimentary, some had fabulous handles – and early pullers can fetch £1000.

The first corkscrew patent was registered in 1795 by vicar Reverend Samuel Henshall. His design was the first to have a circular cap at the base of a corkscrew, which 'by preventing the Screw from penetrating further, instantly effects the turning round of the Cork.' Get your hands on a genuine Henshall and you have a device that is worth at least £1500. Authentic pieces are inscribed 'Obstando Promoves' ("by standing firm, one advances"), but even copies can fetch £200.

Reverend Henshall's invention sparked off a wave of often-ingenious designs, with more than 300 patents being put forward over the following century for "mechanical" corkscrews. One of the most collectable is the brass double-action corkscrew patented by Sir Edward Thomason in 1802. It had three screws that worked together to pierce, withdraw and then discharge the cork. Examples with the motto 'Ne Plus Ultra' and decorated barrels can be picked up for between £300 and £600 – though rare examples with gilded serpent handles have hit £7000. It originally sold for a guinea. Period copies of the Thomason can be picked up for less than £100.

Other design classics include Thomas Lund's rack-and-pinion "bottle grip" of 1838 and the Royal Club, patented by Charles Hull in 1864, which can fetch more than £2000. The King's Screw by the 17th century company Heely is another popular investment, easily recognisable with its side handle and rack-and-pinion. Pieces often go for £300 or more.

Corkscrews touched by royalty also have great appeal. The record price for screws of this nature is the £18,400 paid for an 18th century silver pocket corkscrew engraved with Queen Alexandra's initials, auctioned in 1997.

 # CORK AU VIN

Our Gallic neighbours never having been overly concerned with barbarous Anglo-Saxon things like hygiene, French vintners were characteristically tardy in their adoption of the humble cork. Until well into the 17th century they were content to seal their bottles of exquisite wine with oil-drenched rags – twisted and stuffed into the glass necks – instead.

Prices of classic corkscrews fluctuate but – thanks partly to the growth of demand in the wine market – remain generally strong, and can provide fascinating opportunities for all wallets and palates. The most sought after tend to be those made of silver and those which include hidden accessories – such as knives, or a brush with which to dust off the top of a wine bottle. Top values always go with a maker's name.

Novelty corkscrews are also highly sought after, with devices involving animals, sports or humans the most appealing. The German Steinfield & Reimer design featuring ladies' can-can dancer legs, from the late Victorian era, can fetch between £150 and £350.

Only buy working examples. Damage to old corkscrews, such as cracks in handles, can turn collectable pieces into almost worthless items of slight interest. However, rust can easily be removed, and a spot of oil will bring a seized piece of junk back to life. Be alert for potential fakes – genuine 18th century corkscrews were hand-cut and not always sharp.

FOLLOWING A CORKING IDEA

The International Correspondence of Corkscrew Addicts at www.corkscrewnet.com; The Corkcrew Centre at www.corkscrewcentre.com. Books include *Miller's Corkscrews & Wine Antiques* by Christopher Sykes and Phil Ellis; *Collectable Corkscrews* by Frederique Crestin-Billet.

Cricket

A spirit of adventure among willow-bat-wielding gentlemen hit cricket across the English boundary in the days of the Victorian Empire. The fascinating and detailed history of this popular imperial export has created one of the most sought after sporting investments, in the shape of venerable cricketing bible *Wisden*, amongst other fascinating objects.

Wisden Cricketers' Almanack, which has published all the scorecards of first class matches since 1864, is the cricketing collectable that holds the most appeal among investors. A complete set of *Wisdens* could have been picked up for about £20,000 a decade ago, but in top condition sets go for as much as £100,000 today. Any extra element can help: a set owned by cricket legend W. G. Grace sold for £150,000 in 2005.

One of the most rare is the 1916 edition, as there was a limited print run due to the outbreak of World War I, and it included the obituary of W. G. Grace. However, post-war editions can still be picked up for just a few pounds.

Cricket can be traced to 1550 but it was not until the 17th century that it became an adult sport. The MCC has four cricket scorebooks kept by the first scorer at Lord's – Samuel Britcher – dated 1795 to 1806. They were purchased for £324,000 in 2005.

THE ASHES

At a cricket match at The Oval in 1882, England were beaten for the first time on home soil. A sarcastic obituary ran in *The Sporting Times*, claiming English cricket had died and the body was being cremated, with the ashes going to Australia. At the next Test series in Melbourne a small terracotta urn was given to the England captain as a symbolic joke – and has been played for ever since. The contents are believed to be the ashes of a cricket stump or bail, but might even be those of an Aboriginal cricketer called King Cole, who toured England in 1868. The Ashes are insured for £1m but Australians would happily pay anything for the ownership.

Cricket bats receive understandable affection from collectors, who tend to only be focused on historical artefacts rather than the modern equipment. Anything belonging to W. G. Grace – who played cricket between the 1860s and 1890s – is always of great value, as he inaugurated the modern stature of cricket we know today.

The cricket bat used by W. G. Grace to knock up his first top class century has been valued at £80,000 but is kept under lock and key at Lord's Cricket Club. However, you can still pick up a W. G. Grace letter for a more affordable £500.

A county bat signed by the current side might fetch only £30 while even a recent signed Ashes bat signed by both sides might go for only £300, as so many similar bats are available.

Legendary names and occasions will always hold value. Fred Trueman, Denis Compton and Don Bradman command top price. A "baggy" green cap Bradman wore for his final Test cap in 1948 fetched £175,000 at an auction in 2008.

Any item related to the controversial Bodyline Series of 1932 and 1933 between England and Australia is also a blue-chip bet. The England captain was Douglas Jardine while Herbert Sutcliffe and Wally Hammond were other key players.

Pre-World War I is also a fascinating market. You can still pick up original 1898 photos of the England cricket team for £600 – a marvellous piece of history. Items after 1960 tend not to be so valuable, but are relative bargains. Clothing from recent stars such as Derek Randall and Jack Russell – their blazers, for instance – can usually be bought for less than £400.

HITTING FOR SIX

Buy from a reputable dealer and avoid items made to cash in on events. See also the Cricket Memorabilia Society (www.cricketmemorabilia.org); Marylebone Cricket Club (MCC), Lord's (www.lords.org/mcc). Auctioneers include T. Vennett-Smith, at www.vennett-smith.com.

Cuban Cigars

For cigar aficionados there is no substitute for the best Cuban Havanas, also known in Spanish as *Habanos*. This is because Cuba is the only place where you find the ideal combination of sun, soil and skill to create the perfect cigar.

The best investments tend to be limited editions due to their relatively small supply. One of the recent top bets – as well as greatest smokes – have been the labels of Davidoff and Dunhill, who quit the Cuban market in 1992 and are rare. Had you purchased a box in 1992 for £500 you could now be sitting on an investment worth £5000 and climbing.

But perhaps the most sought after cigars of all are those of the 1492 Humidor, a box of 50 named after the year Christopher Columbus discovered Cuba, and produced under license by the Cuban government in 1992. With a limited edition of 501 boxes they could be picked up for £800 when released but now might fetch £14,500.

There are 33 separate Havana brands, offering more than 240 different cigars, with plenty of names to capture the attention of investors. Classic Cuban labels such as Partagas, Cohiba, Ramon Allones and Bolivia never go out of favour.

The limited editions are often just produced for specific countries, with Britain being a top destination renowned for its stringent English Market Selection (EMS) control.

Although Americans smoke more Cuban cigars than anywhere else it officially bans imports from its tyrannical little neighbour.

Novice cigar smokers might first be tempted by more mellow offerings from great names, such as Romeo Y Julieta or Monte Cristo. The latter boasts the best-selling cigar in the world – a Petit Corona sized "No.4", which sells for a tenner.

Investors purchase in boxes of 25 or cabinets of 50 and store them in humidors to keep them from drying out and losing flavour. Small storage humidors can be purchased for as little as £50 although specialist merchants can look after them in more controlled environments. Cigars are kept at 68 degrees Fahrenheit and 67% humidity to replicate the Cuban climate. Cigars can enjoy a shelf life of 50 years and mellow with age.

Investors typically purchase two identical boxes of merchandise – one to lay down and sell at least three years later at a profit, and the other to light and enjoy going up in smoke.

MAIDEN'S THIGHS

It is a myth that cigars are rolled on the inside of a maiden's thighs, but true that skilled women pile leaves on their laps when sorting out the best tobacco. The cured leaves are then later handled by the Torcedores – expert cigar-rollers.

Size really does matter for the cigar connoisseur. The Cuban term for cigar size is "vitola" and the biggest is Gran Corona, which is nine and a quarter inches long with a cigar ring gauge of 47 – a 47/64 of an inch diameter.

Each brand has its own characteristic flavour, but different vitolas vary the taste. The bigger cigars can offer rich but cooler smokes, while fat cigars tend to burn more slowly and provide a fuller flavour.

A cigar cutter or scissors are also essential. It is a schoolboy error to bite the head off – *la perilla* – like a Clint Eastwood tough guy. The ideal draw is normally found with a clean cut an eighth of an inch from the end of the cigar.

SMOKING HOT INVESTMENTS

The Association of Independent Tobacco Specialists in Cardiff provides details of local traders and smoking groups, contact via www.uktobacco.co.uk. Tobacconists are exempt from the smoking ban and you can still enjoy a puff on their premises within the law. Websites www.cigars-review.org and www.habanos.com are a great source of information.

Dan Dare

'Pilot of the Future' Dan Dare and his loyal batman Digby first blasted off into outer space to fight the green egg-headed Mekon from Venus almost 60 years ago. Much of his future is already history but prices for the *Eagle* comics, in which his adventures first appeared, really would be something from science fiction to schoolboy fans who bought them originally for mere pocket money.

A 3d (thruppence) edition of the first comic from April 1950 is now worth at least £850 if it is still in pristine condition, while a full set of his swashbuckling exploits can fetch thousands of pounds. On top of this there is a whole raft of Fifties Dan Dare memorabilia – from board games to ray guns – that has more than tripled in value over the past decade.

 ANTI-GRAVITATIONAL UPPER LIP

Dan's appeal is the gentle stiff-upper-lipped code of conduct where heroes played by the rules and only disabled their foes with stun guns rather than slaughtering them in vast and bloody killings. In truth, it offered nostalgia for a lost past rather than any realistic taste of the future.

Dan Dare was seen as embodying the next generation of the RAF for when, after victory in World War II, Britain would surely go on to conquer space. The adventures were a wholesome antidote to the hard boiled comic strips coming over from the US. Lush artwork by original artist Frank Hampson was a key part of the appeal, too.

The exciting storylines often seem to say more about traditional family values and post-war Britain than the actual future, which only adds to their attraction for many modern age readers.

At its height almost a million copies of *Eagle* were printed a week so there are plenty of examples on the market. Condition is the primary consideration for collectors. A mint condition first issue might be worth up to £850 but a well-read example can still be picked up for about £50. Later issues cost far less. Only Dan Dare from the Fifties and Sixties is seriously collectable.

Eagle was a large comic and would often be folded by the newsagent and thumbed by shoppers before it was even bought. Postmen would also have to crease it up just to get it through the letterbox.

A Dan Dare Ray Gun, complete with noisy sparks and in the original fabulous retro box, may be worth £1400. The same packaged gun was worth about £500 a decade ago. Now even without packaging it may fetch £500.

Another popular weapon is the Dan Dare Planet Gun that fires out plastic rings. It is less rare, though, so top examples may fetch about £130. Other items that are great fun – which really does help boost the value – include the Space Race board game and a Dan Dare belt and tie set, worth £300 and £200 respectively.

The Dan Dare "Eagle" space vehicle was used for taking tourists between Earth, Mars and Venus. It is only nine inches long but worth £600 if still in the original box – and looks fantastic.

PREPARE FOR LIFT OFF

There is no use investing in Dan Dare memorabilia or *Eagle* comics unless you love the character and his adventures. Cheap reprints of his early stories are available in bookshops and can provide a great taster. Comics International publishes details of fairs. Comic Book Postal Auctions can help on trading and valuations (www.compalcomics.com). Websites like www.dandare.org provide *Eagle* details.

Dinky Toys

Dinky Toys can offer big returns for miniature die-cast vehicle enthusiasts. Prices of top collectables have fetched two or three times their estimate at auction in the past year. The record price is £19,975 for a pre-war "type 22" W. E. Boyce delivery van in March 2008. It was among the first made by Dinky after it began as a Meccano spin-off in 1934.

Although the pre-war vehicles may cost thousands, later vehicles made in the Fifties and Sixties tend to be more affordable for the adventurous investor. A Fifties "Guy Van" with iconic livery selling Spratt's dog biscuits may fetch £500 – but if it is Weetabix then expect to get as much as £3000.

However, a later less fashionable "Bedford Van" sporting John Menzies might be picked up for £25 while a relatively modern iconic Ford Capri, currently growing in popularity, can be got for £100.

With more than a thousand different Dinky models made over the years, a guidebook is essential when picking through variations. Each is recognisable thanks to a special manufacturing number on the underside of the vehicle.

The first vehicles were the Modelled Miniatures "22" range of six vehicles, followed by the "23" set of racing cars, "24" set of motor cars and "25" of commercial vehicles. These models immediately captured the hearts of a pre-war generation that had never enjoyed quality metal toy cars before.

Dinky manufacturing was then suspended during the war. Afterwards – from 1949 – there was an explosion in choice, in a toymaker's heyday that lasted well into the Sixties.

The decline of Dinky vehicles unfortunately then echoed that of the British motoring industry, as quality suffered and the company folded in 1979.

TRAIN-ING WHEELS

Dinky Toys were not originally aimed to be played with as toys on their own but were introduced only as accessories to established railway kits offered by parent company Hornby.

Any chips or blemishes in the paintwork can have a huge impact on price, and a well played with car may fetch a tenth of that of a top-notch example. An original box doubles value. Dinky collectables are opposite to the real classic car market, as total restorations can lower the value of the original die-cast find.

The market is littered with frauds and restorations that may require an expert eye to spot. A telltale sign is if the colour looks too fresh – paint loses its lustre over time and this is difficult to fake. Be wary of rare undocumented promotionals – known as code threes – as they are hard to verify.

If you want to make money buy toys that you can't play with. They should be in as-new condition with an original box – and kept that way.

Provenance is key for investors. It is better to purchase vehicles from a reputable dealer with a history than trusting to luck with the internet.

Because there is so much choice, focus on particular areas and age. When enthusiasts collect they tend to do so in sets they wish to complete – bare this in mind.

The oldest vehicles tend to hold highest values as few have survived unscathed, but unique one-off colour schemes can also fetch high prices. Popular genres for collectors include military vehicles, buses, trucks with advertising livery and farm tractors.

Although Matchbox and Corgi toy vehicles can be collectable they tend not to be as valuable as Dinky.

HOT PURSUIT

Two industry must-reads worth studying are *The Great Book of Dinky Toys* and *Dinky Toys and Modelled Miniatures* (out of print, but widely available second-hand), both written by Mike and Sue Richardson.

The Dinky Toy Collectors Association is also a great source of essential information, as are the specialist trade magazines *Model Collector* and *Diecast Collector*. The Collectors Association offers advice and a journal featuring members' articles. Write to DTCA, PO Box 60, Norwich, NR4 7WB. Also check out specialist magazine and publisher *Model Collector*, whose website may be found at www.modelcollector.com.

Dinosaurs

Dinosaur-hunting is big business for real-life adventurers. The most successful is the American maverick Peter Larson who digs away in the western plains of Montana, Wyoming and South Dakota with a mini bulldozer and rifle bayonet.

Larson, who is a palaeontologist from the Black Hills Institute of Geological Research, discovered a 65-million-year-old Tyrannosaurus Rex called "Sue" and sold it as the largest, most complete T-Rex for £4.15m in 1997.

It is a far cry from the early days of Victorian exploration.

The first recorded discovery came when 12-year-old Mary Ann found an Ichthyosaur skeleton in Dorset in 1811. This was followed by Lewes physician Gideon Mantell, and his wife Mary Ann Woodhouse, who found dinosaur teeth in 1822. Such early fossilised curios became highly sought after among 19th century collectors but at the time many were not seen as dinosaur bones – they were thought to come from modern animals like rhinos, or even mythical dragons.

The dinosaur was only given its "terrible lizard" name in 1841 by the first superintendent of the Natural History Museum, Richard Owen. It wasn't until the early 1980s that they once again captured the imagination, for punters as well investors, when dusty old exhibitions were revamped – and then along came the 1993 movie *Jurassic Park*. Since then prices have been soaring and the value of top collectables – such as a Triceratops skull – have risen as much as tenfold over the past decade, from £12,500 to £125,000.

WHEN CHICKENS RULED THE EARTH

If you want to buy a living dinosaur the closest you can get may be a chicken. This is because a popular hypothesis is that dinosaurs evolved into birds. A chicken's physical structure, egg-laying and nurturing characteristics seem to indicate it has some central things in common with the Tyrannosaurus Rex. This is unlike, in fact, the cold-blooded reptile lizards, which waddle splay-legged upon the earth and hug it for warmth. Hens strut about like the king of the dinosaurs may have done.

The daddy of all dinosaurs for investors is the Tyrannosaurus Rex. Even in the macho heavyweight world of dinosaurs the T-Rex is perhaps the most dangerous killing machine that has ever walked the earth. A skull of a Tyrannosaurus was bought by actor Nicholas Cage for £137,094 at auction in 2007, while even a replica of a T-Rex's head is likely to set you back almost £5000.

Prices for other dinosaur bones vary hugely depending on the quality and from which part of the more than 1000 species, that have so far been discovered, it has come from. A Triceratops skeleton sold for £400,000 in 2008 while a prehistoric Siberian mammoth fetched £200,000. A plant-eating Scelidosaurus might go for £100,000 and a marine Ichthyosaur for £24,000.

A well-preserved dinosaur egg sold for £48,460 in 2007 though examples can be found for just a few hundred pounds. Eggshell and bone fragments can still be picked up for pocket money.

DINOSAUR HUNTING

Warning: you break the law if you buy a black market dinosaur smuggled in from abroad, so check with authorities beforehand. Contact the Natural History Museum, www.nhm.ac.uk; Black Hills Institute of Geological Research, www.bhigr.com.

Dr Who

No need to hide behind the sofa when it comes to Dr Who collectables. Since teleporting back on to our TV screens in 2005 after a 16-year break, the 900-year-old Time Lord from Gallifrey has seen the price of related props and merchandise soar reassuringly.

Most sought after of all is the Dalek. An original made out of bits of old wood, sink-plungers and Morris Minor indicators fetched £36,000 in 2005 – not uncoincidentally, when Dr Who returned in his ninth reincarnation as Christopher Eccleston. A couple of decades earlier it was sold for £4,600.

Surviving Sixties toys relating to the Doctor are valuable, as most were thrown away. A 1965 clockwork Cowan, de Groot Dalek, costing the equivalent of 82p when new, is today worth £600 if boxed. A Dalek "swap-its" by Cherilea, sold for 5p, now sells for £100; and a colourful Louis Marx friction-drive Dalek can go for £400 boxed.

Perhaps the most coveted and elusive items are the handful of complete Dalek playsuits that survived a factory fire in the mid-Sixties. A surviving Scorpion blue-suit Dalek costume with flashing eye can change hands for at least £5000.

During the Dr Who wobbly props heyday of the Sixties and Seventies pieces used were often cannibalised and thrown away, which boosts the value of the rare surviving artefacts.

Sadly, many of the most ghoulish foes, including Dalek leader Davros, were not killed by the Doctor, but rotted away as neglected latex rubber. However, old Daleks can still occasionally sell for £10,000 while a Cyberman suit might go for £3000.

Even the original wooden police box Tardis fell apart in the Seventies after all those years of time travel – it had originally been a prop on Dixon of Dock Green. A later Tardis from the Eighties has been valued at more than £100,000.

William Hartnell first stepped out of a police box in 1963, but it is the longest-running Doctor Who, Tom Baker, who presided over the show's popular Seventies era, who has the biggest fan base. His coat fetched £800 at auction more than 20 years ago and is now estimated to be worth more than £20,000. Find one of his plentiful long scarves and you can demand up to £1000.

However, the market is flooded with prop fakes and it is wise not to purchase without making sure the history that can be traced back to the BBC. A good way to spot a fake is, curiously, that the copy is often better made!

LEELA

One of the more unusual Dr Who collectables is a Leela doll, a female sidekick for Tom Baker during the Seventies. Boys shunned the toy as a Barbie Doll look-alike and makers Denys Fisher couldn't even give the doll away. Now she is worth about £300 while the doll of Tom Baker typically fetches £150.

Time will only tell regarding the popularity of the latest Dr Who, Matt Smith (the 11th incarnation), but enthusiasm for recent stars Christopher Eccleston and David Tennant means items relating to them could grow in value in the future.

William Hartnell, Patrick Troughton, Jon Pertwee and Tom Baker have traditionally slugged it out for the most collectable top spot, but for signatures Troughton is the best, often fetching £300, as he rarely took part in promotions.

Later Eighties incarnations of the Doctor have been less popular, but merchandise from the era has the advantage that it can still be purchased at reasonable prices.

TRACKING THE TIME LORD

The Who Shop International (www.thewhoshop.com); Howe's Transcendental Toy Box (www.tardis.tv); and the Doctor Who Appreciation Society (www.dwasonline.co.uk).

Electric Guitars

Vintage electric guitars can be music to the ears for investors wanting to match those riffs with blistering returns – but you may need a rock star's wallet to afford one.

Jazz musician Les Paul invented a solid-body electric guitar in 1941 and this inspired the 1952 Gibson model. The 1959 Gibson Les Paul Standard was the top guitar for musicians like Keith Richards and Jimmy Page during the Sixties.

An original Gibson with the famous sunburst finish can change hands for as much as £250,000 thanks to a mouth-watering combination of rare timbers, craftsmanship and finish.

However, for many the best is a Fender – the Telecaster. Fender Telecaster was launched in 1946, 15 years after the very first hollow-instrument electric guitars by Rickenbacker. Fenders were among the first mass produced electric guitars made. Their clean audio quality has never been surpassed and an early Blackguard Telecaster can cost as much as £50,000 – though usually far less.

But the Fender Stratocaster is the most sought after electric guitar of them all. Eric Clapton's favourite Strat – a 1954 model nicknamed Blackie – fetched £1m at auction in 2005, while another played by Jimi Hendrix in the Sixties is worth £500,000.

Even battered Sixties Strats not touched by rock gods can fetch £20,000. About 30 years ago you could still pick up a 1954 all-original Strat for about £1000. But by 1990 it was worth £35,000 and now might fetch double this amount.

Those not on rock star budgets can opt for a Seventies Gibson L-6S as used by Razorlight's Johnny Borrell, which can still be picked up for less than £1000.

Limited edition reissues of early classic models can also hold their value well.

 ## SCORCHING RETURNS

Jimi Hendrix occasionally set light to guitars before smashing them up. At a London Astoria gig in 1967 this practice hospitalised him with burns. A flame blistered Hendrix Fendo Stratocaster, passed to Frank Zappa, sold for £400,000 in 2002.

It is not just the craftsmanship but the limited numbers in which they were produced and played that hike up values. In Britain it was not possible to buy an American import guitar in the Fifties due to a ban on overseas luxury goods.

Fender went off the boil between 1966 and 1984 when owned by CBS, and standards began to slide, along with those of Gibson guitars. This helped boost the values of older classics. But the best investment of all is the first £100 for a starter guitar and learner pack. There is no point investing in guitars unless you can play them as well. This way if guitar values fall then at least you will have something to express your soulful misery on.

PICK UP A PLECTRUM

To get involved in the market, learn to play. You do not have to be Jimi Hendrix or Eric Clapton – just have a few quid and find some spare time. A local guitar dealership can provide guidance on investment purchases. Be wary of fakes: seek provenance. Check out American magazine *Vintage Guitar* for market and price guide. Visit www.stratcollector.com for specialist information.

Fakes

The shady world of forgeries and counterfeits touches every extraordinary investment in this book. Authenticity is key and fakes explain why there is always a need for homework, trading with reputable dealers, and establishing provenance.

Of course, even the most cautious investor can fall foul of the fraudster, whose example can often be better than the real thing. Yet forewarned is forearmed – it certainly helps in the fight to avoid investments becoming worthless junk.

There is also a curious market in the world of deception, where some fakes are not only valuable but have outperformed their authentic counterparts as long-term investments.

The Shadwell Dock "Billy and Charley's" forgeries of the mid-19th century are among the most valuable. Mudlarks William Smith and Charles Eaton scratched a living on the Thames in London by digging up and selling mediaeval artefacts from the foreshore.

To boost business they started to make their own ancient-looking medallions and badges, dropping them through holes in their pockets to later "discover". A Billy and Charley pilgrim badge – with nonsensical inscription – is far more rare than the real thing, and can fetch £4000 compared to an authentic equivalent worth only about £200.

Forgeries are not just about tricking people out of money – propaganda and a desire to create history are also driving forces. One of the most fascinating is the Skull of Doom.

It is reportedly a holy relic from an ancient 3600-year-old civilisation, dug up during the Twenties in British Honduras by English adventurer Frederick Albert Mitchell-Hedges, and a possible inspiration for the most recent escapades of movie hero Indiana Jones. But despite the quartz skull later being revealed as a 19th century fake it is still heralded as a great find – along with other crystals found – and often displayed at museums. The Smithsonian Institute valued the skull at $500,000 in the Seventies. It has kept a more recent valuation secret to keep the mystery alive – which may boost the price even further.

Perhaps the most famous 20th century fraud was the 'Piltdown Man'. This paleontological hoax was discovered at a gravel pit in Piltdown, East Sussex, in 1912, and heralded as a missing link between monkey and man. Yet in 1953 it was exposed as a forgery made from human and orangutan skull with chimpanzee teeth. The priceless relic was nothing but a collection of worthless old bones.

F FOR FAKE

F stands for fake, as film director Orson Welles pointed out in his 1974 movie on art deception *F for Fake*. Welles, who made his name in 1938 tricking a radio audience into believing a Martian invasion was underway, faked "real" footage of Howard Hughes in this movie about fraud.

One of the world's greatest art swindlers was Han van Meegeren. He took revenge on art critics who had criticised his talents by duping them with scores of forged Dutch master paintings, earning millions of pounds in the process.

The greatest was "The Supper at Emmaus", originally painted by Vermeer. Meegeren's fake sold for 520,000 guilders in 1937 – equivalent to $2.5m today – and was hung in pride of place at the top art museum in Rotterdam.

He was only exposed when arrested for collaboration after the war for selling a Vermeer to Nazi number two Hermann Göring. To vindicate his innocence he had to admit to and prove that he was, in fact, a forger. One of the skills he revealed included baking his art at more than 100 degrees centigrade to give it the appearance of genuine old age.

Meegeren fakes have since risen in value and his con skills have been shown off at international art exhibitions. The picture painted in prison to prove he was a fraudster sold at auction for £20,000 in 1996.

CON TRICK

Fakes are as easy to find as the real thing – and everywhere. Look for a bargain that seems too good to be true, such as a suspicious looking internet sale or dodgy market trade deals. Never forget that fraud is a serious criminal offence. Advice on pursuing valuable fakes can be garnered from books such as *Fake? The Art of Deception* by Mark Jones. See *The Fake: Forgery and Its Place in Art* by Sandor Radnoti, for an introduction to the art-side of this adventurous world of quirky collectables. Auction houses try to avoid fake sales but they occasionally crop up – sometimes even announced. Seek their expert guidance too.

Feudal Titles

If the idea of being treated like nobility puffs out your chest with pride then why not pay for the privilege? No need for brown-envelope bungs to the government, stately marriages, or sucking up to the queen – just go shopping.

Lords of the Manor titles and the occasional baronetcy are often up for grabs at specialist auctions – with prices from £5000 up to more than £100,000. Issued in finite numbers, their value tends to hold or rise over the years, but their biggest return is in good old-fashioned snob appeal.

Buying a lordship is not just about buying a fancy title, as there can also be some interesting extras within the small print that might make it a particularly shrewd investment. They can convey rights to hold markets and fairs, or to extract minerals, collect timber, and fish in the local rivers. The right to fish can be particularly valuable for keen anglers.

On the downside, it is worth checking if you might also be held accountable for repair bills, such as maintaining the village dyke or parish church walls.

 DROIT DU SEIGNEUR

Sales were enabled by the 1922 Law of Property Act, which dispenses with the last vestiges of feudal tenure, although it preserved a few ancient rights. This allows investors to purchase a Lord of the Manor title without the land. It also ensured alleged ancient feudal privileges such as the "droit du seigneur" – a probably mythical right to deflower betrothed virgins – are not thrown in as part of the deal.

Lordship titles have been around for more than a thousand years but it wasn't until William the Conqueror turned up in 1066 that they were handed out like baubles to those who pledged loyalty. In the Domesday Book there were at least 13,418 recorded.

Strictly speaking the feudal lordship is not a noble moniker to put in front of a name – though no one will stop you. Buy a Lord of the Manor, and you should technically strut around as Mr Snooty, Lord of the Manor, rather than simply Lord Snooty.

Barons are a few steps higher up the feudal social ladder from manorial lords, so although baronies might cost more, they bestow the right to call yourself a baron or baroness.

Anyone buying a lordship hoping they enjoy a snooze in the House of Lords should realise the manor titles are not peerages bequeathed by the realm.

The title is a property and should not be purchased until lawyers have checked over the legal paperwork to make sure it is valid. Investors can pay £400 to check small print for buying a genuine title. Auctioned titles come on the market because aristocrats sell them off as spare monikers with little sentimental value. Many families have dozens of titles acquired down the family tree. The Duke of Devonshire owns about 600.

The highest price so far for a lordship was £171,000 for the lordship of the manor of Wimbledon ten years ago. Since then the market has remained fairly stable but a limited supply means prices rarely fall. Irish and Scottish baronies tend to be among the priciest titles, fetching at least £30,000 a piece, thanks to wealthy Americans looking for a dinner party excuse to talk about their rich heritage.

Other cost factors are any area's snob appeal – the Manor of Kensington sold for £117,000 a decade ago, while Kentish Town was a snip at £12,000. Bargain hunters should look at rural villages as suburban sprawls tend to ramp up title prices since more potential buyers live in the area.

Symbolism can play a role. Former boxer Chris Eubank paid £45,000 for the Lordship of the Manor of Brighton, which included feudal rights to 4000 herrings, three cows and a slave every year. He was also buying slave freedom.

 ## JOINING THE NOBS

The Manorial Society of Great Britain has more than 1800 members and is the leading auctioneer of titles, selling up to 300 feudal lordships a year (www.msgb.co.uk); Strutt & Parker also occasionally sells titles, www.struttandparker.com.

Film Posters

Film posters have made blockbuster returns in recent years thanks not only to their collectable appeal but also their fantastic artwork, which can often look as great on the wall as any masterpiece.

The most sought after examples tend to be of older pre-war silver screen movies made in an era when cinema posters were thrown away once the movie closed. Posters for movies that stand the test of time attract the highest values.

Over the past couple of decades, vintage posters previously costing a few hundred pounds have risen to several thousand and continue to climb. Movie fans have therefore started collecting for later films, pushing up their values as well.

The great artwork in posters is what gives these collectables extra special appeal. The 1958 Alfred Hitchcock movie *Vertigo* is one of the best examples, as it boasts iconic artwork by Saul Bass – giving it a value of £5000. The same poster fetched £300 in 1990.

James Bond also has a die-hard following that means values rarely fall. A 1963 *From Russia With Love* poster can sell for £5000 – a couple of decades ago it was only worth £100. This is due to its iconic artwork by Italian artist Renato Fratini.

If the great imagery includes the draw of an iconic Hollywood star – such as old classics like Marilyn Monroe, Humphrey Bogart, Cary Grant, Sean Connery or Audrey Hepburn – you have a blue-chip investment with international market appeal.

Horror and science fiction have proved to be among the best market for movie poster investors in the past because they enjoy an avid fan base that never seems to fade.

The most expensive original film poster to date is an original poster for the 1927 Fritz Lang movie *Metropolis*, sold for $690,000 – almost £400,000 – in 2005. However, if one of only two surviving posters of the 1932 film *The Mummy* starring Boris Karloff was auctioned it might fetch £500,000. A decade ago this poster was worth £250,000.

 ## GRAPEFRUITS OF WRATH

Rarest and most desirable is an original 1931 James Cagney *The Public Enemy* poster, of which no surviving examples are known. The film turned Cagney into a star thanks to a daring "tough guy" performance, where he controversially slapped actress Jean Harlow – and famously shoved a grapefruit in her face at breakfast.

Cult movies tend to maintain value, as there is always strong demand.

Those on tighter budgets might look to modern iconic movies, such as an early example for Quentin Tarantino's 1992 *Reservoir Dogs*, currently worth £500 and rising fast. Others include 1995 computer animated movie *Toy Story*, which can go for £300.

Generally, movie posters are worth more in the original language in which the film was made, and foreign examples of all-time classics such as *Casablanca, Gone With the Wind, The Godfather* and *Citizen Kane* may cost less than £500.

Condition is key for collectors and only the best surviving examples will do. The market is awash with forgeries so it is a good idea to use a reputable dealer or auction house. An original British movie poster tends to be 30 inches in height by 40 inches across, while reprints are often slightly smaller – 29" by 39".

If you spend a couple of hundred pounds on an anti-acidic treatment for a poster to stop it yellowing it is perfectly safe to store it in a frame fronted with UV filtered glass – just so long as it is hung in a dry area out of direct sunlight. This way you can also admire your poster while watching its value grow.

 SILVER SCREEN DREAM

Excellent coffee table guides to capture the imagination include the series of decade books *Film Posters of the 30s*, (and *40s*, *50s*, *60s*, *70s* and *80s*), by Tony Nourmand and Graham Marsh. Traders include The Reel Poster Gallery (www.reelposter.com).

First Edition Books

Bookworms can turn a love of literature into a healthy investment if they look after their novels. Hardback first editions tend to be the best bets and if you pick a future classic up for just a few pounds, the plot may indeed have a happy ending – with the tome being worth thousands in a few years time.

Predicting classic collectables for the future is notoriously difficult but it is no coincidence that timeless investments tend to be those that are still a great read today. An 1816 first edition of Jane Austen's *Emma* sold for a record-breaking £180,000 at auction in 2008. Another classic, an 1847 *Wuthering Heights* by Emily Brontë, sold for £114,000 in 2007.

The earlier the book by an author, the more it tends to be worth. This is because print runs would have been far smaller when they were unknown, as opposed to when they became bestsellers.

A first edition of an early J. K. Rowling *Harry Potter* book can fetch five figures, while later first editions in the series change hands for (relatively speaking) mere hundreds of pounds. One of the first 500 signed hardback copies of the J. K. Rowling book *Harry Potter and the Philosopher's Stone* sold for £10.99 in 1997, while a decade later the same sold at auction for £27,370. An unsigned first edition may go for £10,000 at auction.

H. G. Wells was already an established author when his 1897 science fiction hit *The Invisible Man* came out so first editions can still be found for £400. Meanwhile, 1898 *War of the Worlds* may cost (again, relatively speaking) only £800.

The transfer of print adventures to the big screen always boosts values.

Look at valuable or potentially valuable books as an investment and not something to read – any nicks or creases only lower the value. Buy a cheap copy to enjoy but put the pristine condition copy away under lock and key.

Most important of all for investment purposes is the dust jacket, as few examples of old books stand the test of time with the cover still intact. A 1938 first edition of *Brighton Rock* by Graham Greene with original jacket can fetch £30,000. However, a well-thumbed copy of the same book, that has seen better days, might sell for just £500.

FIRST-SPOTTING

To identify a first edition, phrases like 'new edition' and 'this edition' are meaningless. Investors should look for 'first published' and 'first printed' dates – look in the copyright, or "verso" page, for help.

Top collectable genres include children's classics, crime writing and science fiction. Queen of the whodunnit is Agatha Christie. Her first Poirot novel, *The Mysterious Affair at Styles*, was published in 1921, and a first edition is now worth up to £20,000. It is hard to imagine she will ever go out of fashion.

A 1930 first edition of hard-boiled detective novel *The Maltese Falcon* by Dashiell Hammett with original dust jacket can fetch £50,000 – thanks to the film noir appeal of the classic movie of the book.

The Tale of Peter Rabbit by Beatrix Potter from 1901 can fetch £40,000, even without a dust jacket; while a 1937 first edition of *The Hobbit* by J. R. R. Tolkien may cost £20,000.

A classic orange Penguin book might be a good place to start — and it is also a good budget choice. These iconic editions ran from the mid-Thirties to the late Fifties. The first run was of *Ariel* by André Maurois in 1935, copies of which are now worth £60.

 ## INVESTOR BOOKMARKS

The Antiquarian Booksellers Association has a strict code of code practice among members and is worth seeking out if you wish to ensure you are dealing with a reputable trader (see www.abainternational.com). See also the online bookseller AbeBooks (www.abebooks.co.uk).

Fishing Tackle

Fishing is a hunting skill that stretches back thousands of years, but it was not until the Middle Ages in Britain that the rod – known as the "angle" – gave birth to the gentlemanly sport and pastime, angling.

Tackle collectables start in the 18th century, when the art of making fishing equipment was becoming a highly skilled process involving early reels – known as winches – made of wood. By the 19th century, these reels were being handcrafted by clockmakers skilled at filing pins and making fine grooves. The devices were more elaborate and made of brass and silver attachments.

The most famous is Hardy Brothers, which introduced reel innovations to the market when The Tackle Company was founded by William Hardy in Alnwick, Northumberland, in 1872. Examples of the Hardy Perfect reel range go from under £100 to £2000 or more. However, an investor paid as much as £48,800 for a pair of Hardy White Whickham big-game reels – although this was an unusual one-off.

Other great 19th century reel makers include Illingworth and Aerial reels by Samuel Allcock of Redditch, whose reels change hands for at least £500, while wooden Nottingham reels are also collectable.

Another famous 18th century winch maker to look for is Onesimus Ustonson.

THE ONE THAT GOT AWAY

Perhaps the greatest to get away was the Redmire Monster carp at Bernithan Lake on the Welsh border in 1980. There were several sightings and it appeared to be at least four feet long – with photographic evidence. Sadly, it was never caught and weighed. The world record carp is 88lb 6oz for a giant caught in France in 2007. This fish was exactly four feet long. The British record is 65lb 14oz for the carp Two Tone caught at Conningbrook Lake near Ashford, Kent.

Other tackle investments include rods, lures, trout and salmon flies, as well as willow fishing baskets known as creels, stuffed fish in cabinets and angling books.

Victorian fishing spoons and lures can be of breathtaking beauty and are highly collectable. Examples such as a Gregory lure known as the Wheeldon Spinner, with articulated scaled body and glass eye, sell for more than £1000. Investors can hand over £400 for antique fly wallets complete with gut-eyed salmon flies.

Prices for a quality fish in a case start at about £300, although you can invest four figures if you buy a top name such as J. Cooper and Sons. Rods are more usually purchased for use and it tends to be the early examples with silver

fittings or unusual history that are collectable. Investment-quality rods start at about £200.

The first book on fishing in English is *A Treatyse of Fysshynge wyth an Angle*, published in 1496 by a nun. The famous *Fly Fishing by J. R. Hartley* was fiction for a TV advert but it proved such a hit that an actual book was later published. A far better investment to hunt for is a 1910 edition of Frederic Halford's *Modern Development of the Dry Fly*, which can sell for £4000.

 ## ANGLING FOR A BITE

Do your homework – and use it as a great excuse for fishing. Books include *Classic and Antique Fly-fishing Tackle* by A. J. Campbell; *Fishing Tackle: A Collector's Guide* by Graham Turner; *Antique Fishing Tackle* by Silvio Calabi. Specialist auction houses holding fishing sales include Mullock's (www.mullocksauctions.co.uk).

Football

Football fans can share their devotion off as well as on the field with soccer memorabilia. And unlike the expense and heartache that often goes with team support, this investment could be richly rewarded.

In the past decade the most sought after football programmes have more than doubled in value. The price of other rare items, including medals, caps and shirts, have also shot up and can sell for thousands of pounds.

Manchester United items are the most collectable. Liverpool, Arsenal, Newcastle United, Chelsea, Tottenham Hotspur and Manchester City are among the others with highly sought after memorabilia. But collectable does not always mean valuable.

Small clubs with diehard fans can also push up prices of cherished mementos.

Historic significance is of vital consideration for football investors and this is why the value of the very oldest football programmes can do well, especially around the time of the formation of the Football League in 1888.

Football programmes were not printed until the 1890s, by teams such as Sheffield United, Sheffield Wednesday and Preston North End. Before, in the 1880s, teams like Walsall Town Swifts and Newton Heath (later Manchester United FC) sold cardboard match cards with names and positions on a 1-2-3-5 formation.

A single-sheet team selection when the early Red Devils played Walsall at The Chuckery on November 8th, 1890 – the site before Old Trafford was built – cost 1d on the day but can now fetch £10,000.

Another rarity is anything from the Man United 1958 fixture against Wolverhampton Wanderers, which never took place. The previous week the Munich air disaster killed eight of the Busby Babes and the programmes were destroyed. Saved copies fetch £5000.

FA Cup finals hold special appeal. The first FA Cup final was The Wanderers (amateur footballers from Battersea) versus the Royal Engineers in 1872, but there are no surviving mementos other than the 1-0 score line in favour of The Wanderers.

In 1889/90 Arsenal made it to the regional London FA Challenge Cup Final. They lost 1-0 to Old Westminster but a finalist's medal recently sold for £5000. Key to its appeal is that on it they are still recorded as Royal Arsenal and based south of the river in Plumstead.

The cup wasn't played at Wembley until 1923. A first Wembley final programme cost 3d but can sell for £1000. A year later the price leaped to a shilling as it had a colour front. This Newcastle versus Aston Villa programme is rarer and can go for £6000. The most collectable is the 1915 FA Cup "khaki" Chelsea verses Sheffield United final at Old Trafford, which can change hands for £15,000 – it was the last match played for four years because of World War I.

The highest price ever paid for any FA Cup football memorabilia was £478,000 in 2005 for the oldest surviving Cup, dating back to 1896.

BEWARE OF THE BALL

A pre-1950s leather ball signed in fountain pen by players can hold its value, but in the modern era clubs sign hundreds of balls a year. Some are not even worth kicking about on a pitch as they are only souvenir quality and not constructed to match standard.

The first World Cup final was Uruguay against Argentina in 1930. Uruguay won 4-2 and the winners' medal of their captain José Nasazzi was recently valued at £30,000.

A decade ago a used set of ten 1966 Word Cup Final tickets fetched £1500. This caused football fans to rummage around in their attics for old stubs and swamp the market. You can now buy the same set of used tickets for £450.

Replica signed shirts should be kicked into touch but historic match clothes worn by legends can be solid investments. The hat-trick shirt worn by England footballer Geoff Hurst in the 1966 World Cup final went under the hammer for £91,750 in 2000 – it might fetch double this value if sold now.

A shirt worn by Brazilian soccer legend Pele in the 1970 World Cup final in Mexico fetched £157,000 in 2002.

SOCCER SKILL TIPS

Buy from reputable dealers who guarantee refunds if forgeries are discovered – the modern market is flooded with fakes. Specialist auctioneers include Sportingold Ltd (www.sportingold.co.uk) and T. Vennett-Smith (www.vennett-smith.com).

Fountain Pens

Every great adventurer has a weakness for the gentle art of letter writing. Computer emails and telephone texts have a place, but for written communication there is no substitute for ink and paper. The fountain pen, with its elegant personal flourish, is unique.

The top end of the fountain pen market has seen prices double over the past decade but less expensive examples have suffered in recent years due to the market being opened up with internet sales. However, prices now seem to have stabilised and there are some great classic vintage fountain pens available, with serious collectable appeal. Prices start from about £100.

The golden age of fountain pen collectables is the 1920s and 1930s. The earlier rare "eye-dropper" pens – filled with a bottle using a pipette – tend to hold less appeal for the modern investor.

The Rolls Royce of the market is the Japanese Namiki and Dunhill Namiki, which use the ancient technique of decorative lacquering known as *maki-e*. Collectables can go for £1000 or more. The highest price paid for a fountain pen to date is £183,000 for a Dunhill Namiki "double dragon" maki-e lacquer pen, paid in 2000. It was hand-painted by the Japanese artist Shogo in 1928.

Less expensive but still highly sought after collectables include those by Parker, Waterman, Montblanc and Conway Stewart. Others worth looking at include Sheaffer, Mabie Todd and British De La Rue. These pens go for anything from under £100 to more than £1000 depending, not just on look and age, but the condition and rarity value. This means that details such as unusual extra engravings, artistic designs and colours have a huge impact on prices being paid.

One of the first collectables is the 1921 Parker Big Red Duofold, among the first to write without the risk of leaving a big accidental blob of ink on the page. These can be picked up for about £100, although a mint condition boxed example might go for £500. When first introduced they cost $7, which was equal to an average worker's monthly wages.

 ## PIG'S BLADDERS

The history of fountain pens dates back to the 17th century, when writers scratched around with quills. By the mid-19th century there were primitive fountain pens using pig's bladders to control the flow of ink. However, it wasn't until an insurance salesman called Lewis Waterman lost an important sale because his fountain pen squirted its contents all over his client's application form that a more practical invention arrived. Waterman patented a fountain pen in 1884 that allowed ink to flow without a vacuum forming, thereby enabling smooth and reliable writing.

The history of the modern fountain pen began in 1939 with the launch of the Parker 51, still a great useable writing instrument today and available for less than £200.

Modern limited editions by firms such as Montblanc also have collectable appeal. A Montblanc Hemingway cost £380 when released in 1992 but can now change hands for as much as £1800.

Some vintage pens can be bought for less than their modern counterparts. An 18 carat gold Parker 51 pen and pencil set from the Sixties can be snapped up for £1000, while a modern one is £5000.

PUT PEN TO PAPER

Do your homework. Books include *Fountain Pens: Vintage and Modern* by Andreas Lambrou; *Fountain Pens* by Jonathan Steinberg; *Collectable Fountain Pens* by Juan Manuel Clark. Dealers include Battersea Pen Home (www.penhome.co.uk) and Penfriend (www.penfriend.co.uk).

Gold

Gold has traditionally been an investment for the adventurous. A century ago prospectors would travel the world and risk everything for the chance to strike it rich with this precious metal.

These days – especially in times of economic uncertainty – it provides intrinsic value to which investors like to flee. It is a tangible and permanent asset that always holds its worth – be it as bullion bars, coins, and jewellery or in industry.

The price of gold has quadrupled over the past decade to as high as $1000 a troy ounce. However, in the Nineties the value of gold hardly moved while the stock market soared so the future for gold is unpredictable.

Gold bars (known as bullion) come in many shapes, with purity levels stamped on to the ingot along with a registration number. A typical 400 ounce bar (12.5kg) is known as a London Good Delivery bar.

But most investors usually buy coins. It may cost 3% more per ounce than if buying in bullion bars, but they are far easier to trade. One ounce Krugerrands or quarter-ounce British Sovereigns are among the most popular and can be purchased over the counter at a bullion dealership. The gold price is quoted in US dollars per troy ounce, slightly heavier than a normal ounce (a troy ounce is about 31 grams).

Investors can expect to pay a premium for coins over the current gold market "spot price" of at least 5% and take a hit of as much as 2% when trading them in. No VAT is payable on investment gold. A High Street bank can look after the gold in a safety deposit box for a typical fee of £25 a year.

PANNING FOR WELSH GOLD

Snowdonia in north Wales is as good a place as any in Britain to catch gold fever. Gold is heavy and normally follows the quickest route through a meandering river, depositing in flecks and nuggets at turns. Dig into the silt at the edge of a river and shovel it into a pan with "riffles" at the front designed to catch specks of gold. Carefully swish, discarding any stone, and slowly washing away the smaller particles of sand. Because gold is heavy it should remain at the bottom of the pan and not be washed out. Retire at the end of the day, wealthy.

If you want to invest in gold because you think it is a beautiful asset then buy some jewellery for your partner and enjoy it that way instead. Gold is too soft to be used as jewellery on its own and must be alloyed with other metals. To make white gold it is necessary to add palladium and nickel.

Purity is measured in karats – not to be confused with the weight "carats" used for diamonds. 24k contains 999 parts pure gold per thousand. If less than 24k it is an alloy, with the remainder consisting of metals such as copper, silver or zinc.

Another way to invest in gold is through a fund. There are a couple of specialist UK-based gold funds – one of the most popular is offered by Merrill Lynch – that also gamble on the mining of the precious metal.

Investors can dabble in gold futures and options, too. Bullion can likewise be bought through Gold Bullion Securities Limited, listed on the London Stock Exchange.

There is at least 38,000 tonnes of gold still in the ground worldwide. About 147,000 tonnes of gold has been mined and a fifth of this lies in central banks.

PURSUING THE END OF
THE RAINBOW

You can invest in gold in a variety of ways – consider them all carefully before deciding if the precious metal is for you. Sources of help include the British Numismatic Trade Association (www.numis.co.uk) and the World Gold Council (www.gold.org).

Golf

Those who hanker after a gentler age when you could enjoy a stroll around the countryside in plus fours, swinging clubs about before dinner, might like to invest in golf. Fortunately, a single figure handicap is not essential; but potential adventurous investors still need a sharp eye and steady aim if they are going to make a worthwhile investment shot.

The market took a hit in the late Eighties following a boom partly created by fanatic Japanese golf collectors. This boom went to bust when the Japanese economic bubble duly burst. But now investors are coming back.

Historic artefacts from the 18th century are among the most sought after, with the record price for a metal-blade putter, dating from that era, being £106,000 in 1998. After golf clubs, the balls themselves are also in high demand, with the top price paid to date being £29,900 for a 1902 Henry's Rifled Ball, also bid in 1998.

And while the very earliest pieces of golfing nostalgia may cost thousands of pounds there are plenty of 20th century opportunities to invest in that are still a relative bargain.

Golf began in Scotland in the 14th century. Until the 19th century, clubs were long nosed, wooden and custom made. Irons were only occasionally put in the golf bag for getting out of the heavy rough.

The old golf balls were known as "featheries", stuffed with feathers and sewn in cow's hide with wax thread. These cost the equivalent of £100 a ball so only the wealthy could afford to lose a ball around the course. These days a feather-stuffed ball can fetch as much as £10,000.

In the mid-19th century a "gutty" ball of black gutta-percha rubber from Malaysia was introduced. These heavier but cheaper balls split old-fashioned wooden clubs – thus mass-produced iron-headed clubs began. The gutta balls can sell for £2000 to £4000 at auction.

The 18th and 19th century golf clubs tend to be the most collectable, with long-nosed clubs by makers such as R. Forgan, Alex Patrick and McEwan changing hands for £2000 or more. Perhaps the most sought after, though, are those made by 19th century craftsman Hugh Philp. His clubs can go for at least £4000 each. However, perfectly useable hickory clubs of the era can be picked up for less than £50 each, and enable investors to enjoy playing a round of the historical game as originally intended.

As any golfer will tell you, the putter is the most important tool in the armoury; or rather, the ability to use one with skill. The sport was revolutionised by the development of the "PING" putter in the Sixties. If you stumble across an original 1-A model – which looks like two tuning forks glued together – you may have an investment worth more than £3000. In the early Nineties the putter was a tenth of this price.

Other modern classics include the limited edition Scotty Cameron clubs used by Tiger Woods to win the Masters in 1997. These were initially sold for £2500 but now can go for more than five-figure sums.

19ᵗʰ HOLE

The 19th hole is the name given to the bar at the clubhouse after a full 18 hole round. Although modern golfers may joke about its name, this fictitious hole is actually the reason the sport took off. Rich gentlemen in the 18th and 19th century played golf as an excuse for exercise before a hearty dinner and drink.

Early 20th century golf clubs are still relatively affordable. Clubs stamped with legendary British Open champions of the era – such as Harry Vardon and James Braid – can still be picked up for about £100.

Calendars with golfing scenes from this period can also be picked up for a couple of hundred pounds, while programmes from Open championships might fetch four-figures, depending on the date.

Golf postcards, cigarette cards, china and advertising items can still be found relatively cheaply at antique fairs and auctions.

TEEING OFF

There are regular specialist auctions and sales. The British Golf Collectors' Society promotes the history and tradition of golf collectables (www.britgolfcollectors.wyenet.co.uk).

Gramophone Players

The hi-fi was born when Thomas Edison invented the phonograph in 1877, with the first ever recording being "Mary Had a Little Lamb". The earliest tinfoil phonographs offer a terrible sound but are priceless museum pieces.

However, in 1887 Emile Berliner invented the first commercially available gramophone. It was aimed at the nursery rather than the parlour room. An 1893 Berliner Gramophone might fetch £10,000 today.

Until the 20th century the bulky cylinder players of Edison and Colombia Records provided much of the music entertainment rather than 78 rpm spinning discs. These machines were out of the price reach for most households who had to put a penny into a restaurant or music hall's device if they wanted to enjoy its music. A coin-slot 1898 Colombia Graphophone can sell for £2200. However, it is the later gorgeous looking external horns of gramophones playing 78s that tend to attract most attention as they can make great pieces of furniture as well as being fascinating and historical music machines.

NIPPER ON A COFFIN

Emile Berliner coined "His Master's Voice" (HMV) after seeing an 1899 Francis Barraud painting of Nipper the dog listening to an Edison Bell phonograph. The canine is sitting on a coffin in which his dead owner lies; the phonograph is playing a record of this deceased master's voice to placate the poor creature's sorrow. Berliner airbrushed the coffin and repainted the player as a gramophone to create the iconic advertising logo.

The Berliner Gramophone company used His Master's Voice as the trademark of Johnson's Victor talking Machine in 1901. This highly sought after so-called "Trade-Mark" model can cost £2000.

But HMV then followed a different route to many competitors by tucking the horn behind grills inside oak stand-up models. Such pre-war models can be picked up relatively cheaply as pieces of furniture for the modern house, with a 1911 bow-fronted aspidistra HMV Bijou Grand available for as little as £350 today.

The external horned gramophone reached its zenith in the work of British firm EMG and offspring EM Ginn. They were responsible for huge papier-mâché horns of sizes up to an incredible 36 inches in diameter. An early Thirties EMG model XB gramophone player can sell for £2700 for more.

After World War I the installation of electricity in houses meant mains powered machines became more popular in the home than hand-cranked wind-up models. This allowed for the development of the clear, warm sounding valve radiograms – combining record players with radios – that still sound great today.

It also led to hand-wound models being more focused on the niche portable market for compact small suitcase sized players. These were designed to be equally at home out on a picnic as in the parlour. The iconic HMV portable gramophones of the Twenties and Thirties come in brightly coloured leather boxes, providing a great place to start for novice investors at prices of about £200. They were originally £6 – three weeks' average wages.

GOING FOR A SPIN

Old gramophone players are not designed to just sit in a corner and be admired but need to be taken for a spin. Invest in a box of steel needles – those on machines need to be replaced after just a few plays of a record.

Get expert advice on authenticity before handing over any cash in a serious investment, as many players have non-original bits that dramatically affect values. Look for the original name inside the carriage lid, and make sure it tallies up with the logo on the sound box and tone arm. Drilled holes that look redundant should raise alarm bells. Make sure it can play a record all the way through.

Check out the British Vintage Wireless and Television Museum (www.bvwm.org.uk); British Vintage Wireless Society (www.bvws.org.uk); Howard Hope Gramophones & Phonographs (www.gramophones.uk.com); and The City of London Phonograph and Gramophone Society (www.clpgs.org.uk).

Grandfather Clocks

Time really can be money with grandfather clocks. The past five years has seen a fall in market values due to a change in furniture tastes but this may provide an investment opportunity, as their values tend to go in cycles. A grandfather clock costing £1000 today might have been found for just £20 about 30 years ago. The same clock might have fetched £2500 at its peak.

Investment level grandfathers tend to start at about £1000 but it is not unreasonable to expect to pay more than £10,000 for a top quality clock with a good name.

The grandfather clock – more correctly known as a long-case clock – came to Britain in the 17th century, after the pendulum had been invented in Holland. Famous master craftsmen, such as Thomas Tompion, Joseph Knibb, Dan Quare and George Graham, developed the clock into a finely tuned piece of furniture, whose heyday was in the Georgian era.

Their skills were spread nationwide by other gifted clock makers such as Joseph Finney from Liverpool, Thomas Lister from Halifax, Osborne & Wilson of Birmingham, and Sam Harley of Shrewsbury. However, these are just a few names among scores of top makers across the country, stretching from London to Wales, the Midlands, Manchester, Liverpool and Yorkshire.

SEX CHANGE TIME

The average grandfather clock stands seven feet in height but once it slips below six feet six inches it is deemed to have changed sex and becomes a grandmother clock.

When looking for a quality grandfather clock use your eyes – if proportions look right then your intuition may well serve you well. Check out the dial for telltale signs of fixing; clock hands and faces that have been replaced can hit the value hard. Early examples tend to have brass faces.

A rule-of-thumb Georgian age test is to see if the interior goes all the way to the base or has the generally not-so-early false bottom. The Victorian era still spawned some great Grandfather clock makers but styles became increasingly fussy and cumbersome, making them generally less collectable.

Most of the older clocks were made out of oak but in the 18th century mahogany, which had previously been brought over as boat ballast by sailors returning from the Caribbean, also started to be used.

A grandfather that looks battered and rather basic is not necessarily badly made, but could just be an example using a rustic country style of carpentry – something actually sought after.

A non-working clock is still perfectly collectable but spending a few hundred pounds getting it authentically fixed is money well spent.

Counterfeits and bodged restorations mean five-figure investments can be little more than expensive firewood if you don't do further homework. Experts typically charge about £50 to check out the authenticity and dating of clocks: a worthwhile investment as it is an art the novice is unlikely to get right.

You don't have to be driven crazy by hourly chimes throughout the night as clocks can easily be dampened, although the "tick-tock" can be therapeutic. Early examples often need to be wound up by pulling a weight once a day.

CLOCK ON

Definitive books include out-of-print *English Domestic Clocks* by Cescinsky and Webster; *Grandfather Clocks and their Cases* by Brian Loomes. Shop around antique dealers and visit auction houses.

Grand Pianos

Tickling the ivories can create sweet music for piano investors, with a boom in demand for grands seeing prices soar as much as 200% in the past decade.

The piano hit its lowest note in the 1960s when thousands were destroyed during bizarre charity "piano smashing" events that swept across the nation. But now a yearning for bygone values and renewed musical interest in piano playing is slowly bringing the market back to life – especially for upmarket grands.

While concert grand pianos can fetch as much as £90,000 there are still plenty of decent second-hand gems available for £1000 or less.

Grands are the most collectable due to rarity and better acoustics. Big names like Steinways, and the three Bs – Bechstein, Bluthner and Bösendorfer – offer top investments that rarely fall in value. A top quality 1930s parlour Bechstein grand may cost £3000, while if you want to purchase a Steinway expect to hand over at least £10,000 for a decent example.

Specially commissioned "art case" pianos can be more expensive but more collectable. Uniquely engraved Steinways can go for £50,000 and Strohmengers have fetched £28,000. Other piano investments to look out for include Grotrian-Steinwegs, made by an early family offshoot of the Steinways, and modern Faziolis.

Collectable cachet can also be improved if one of the previous owners who sat at the piano stool was famous. The record-breaker is a 1970 Steinway upright used by John Lennon to write "Imagine", which was snapped up for £1.45m by George Michael a few years ago. Liberace favoured Baldwin pianos and a unique chromium-plated concert grand of his fetched £200,000 – not including the candelabras.

An Elton John upright A-Day Birdcage sold for £91,000 three years ago – it was just one of the many he has owned in his life.

BIRTH OF THE PIANO

The "pianoforte" – meaning soft-loud – was invented in 1709 by Italian Bartolomeo Cristofori, who tinkered with a harpsichord to give it hammer volume control. Only three examples of Cristofori pianos survive and these are now priceless museum pieces not to be played.

The best value pianos tend to be found at auctions, but piano shops are great for providing expert advice on purchase as well as quality instruments.

No matter what piano you purchase it can be a costly disaster unless you have it checked over by a professional piano tuner or specialist adviser first.

Central heating can do particularly terrible damage to pianos if the instrument is not protected or serviced. It can cost up to £10,000 to completely renovate a decent piano. To avoid ruining investment, potential pianos should be professionally tuned at least once a year, and any accidental liquid spills should be tackled immediately.

For those seeking an investment, grand pianos have traditionally been the best buy – but they require a spare 9ft length of space plus room for a potential virtuoso.

The so-called parlour or boudoir grand is typically between 5ft and 7ft long, and can be more practical for moderate sized homes. A baby grand can be as little as 4ft long but the smaller models compromise on bass sound and a quality upright may offer better value for money.

TICKLING THE IVORY INVESTMENTS

Among the specialist piano traders is Piano Auctions Ltd (www.pianoauctions.co.uk); Bonhams also has a piano department (www.bonhams.com). Piano Gen provides information at www.uk-piano.org/piano-gen. Famous piano maker Steinway & Sons can be found at www.steinway.com.

James Bond

The enduring appeal for investors is that, true to the old adage, men still just want to be James Bond.

In recent years the value of 007 related memorabilia has continued rising, helped in part by the latest muscle-bound Daniel Craig reincarnation. However, it is Sean Connery who is the benchmark investment by which all others are measured – and which all others can never quite match. This goes for his baddies and Bond girls, too.

The top price ever reached by a James Bond prop is £1.1m, paid in 2006 for the gadget-packed Aston Martin DB5 driven in both *Goldfinger* and *Thunderball*.

The deadly steel-rimmed frisbee bowler hat donned, and tossed murderously about, by Oddjob – real name Harold Sakata – in *Goldfinger*, made £62,000 a decade ago. And when Ursula Andress stepped out of the sea as Honey Rider in 1962 movie *Dr No* it not only set pulses racing but helped her bikini sell for £44,000 in 2001.

Provenance is key when buying bond movie props. For example, a Pierce Brosnan Brioni suit that he donned in *GoldenEye* hit £16,000 at auction in 2007. But a pair of lace knickers allegedly worn by the actress Shirley Eaton as she lay painted-to-death in *Goldfinger* was valued at £300, as it was not possible to prove they were the real article.

BOND, MCBOND

James Bond is not English, but considers himself Scottish – like Sean Connery. The fictional character was born in Germany to a Scottish father and Swiss-French mother. Bond was orphaned aged 11 when they both died in a mountain climbing accident in Aiguilles Rouges in the French Alps.

First editions by author Ian Fleming are particularly sought after. Bond's first outing in *Casino Royale* is the most valuable. A hardback with dust jacket was worth £1000 two decades ago but now – the centenary of Fleming's birth – £24,000. There is also a market for Bond books by other authors. A top-notch first edition *GoldenEye* by John Gardner can change hands for up to £1500.

James Bond movie posters have been the most successful collectable, rising as much as tenfold in value over the past decade. The attraction is not just that you get to own an iconic poster but great artwork as well. *Dr No* posters go for between £3000 and £8000 depending on condition. A dozen years ago they traded for £200. The iconic 1963 *From Russia With Love* as portrayed by Italian artist Renato Ratini changes hands for up to £5000. Posters of George Lazenby's sole outing in the 1969 *On Her Majesty's Secret Service* have tripled in value to £950 in the last ten years, while the 1974 poster for *The Man with the Golden Gun*, starring Roger Moore, is up from £50 to £500.

JUNK BONDS

Connery is followed by Pierce Brosnan and George Lazenby for collectable appeal. Daniel Craig is fast becoming a favourite but Roger Moore and Timothy Dalton lag behind. David Niven, who played 007 in a spoof Bond film named after but not based on *Casino Royale*, is not considered a real Bond.

Other Bond collectables include vintage toys in original boxes. A 1965 Corgi replica of an Aston Martin DB5 – complete with ejector seat – as used in *Goldfinger* can fetch £300 and set of six 007 Action Man figures go for £1000.

ESPIONAGE INVESTORS

Fan groups that can offer advice include www.mi6.co.uk, Absolutely James Bond (www.ajb007.co.uk), and the James Bond International Fan Club (www.007.info). Trading information is also available at www.bondandbeyond.com and www.007magazine.co.uk. See also *James Bond Movie Posters: the Official 007 Collection*, by Tony Nourmand.

Jeans

Warning. Not everyone looks good in jeans.

I f the mirror tells you that other attire would be more your thing, then pursue that instead. An adventurous investor should be prepared to wear the fashionably-cut merchandise.

However, for those whose derriere enjoys the denim mould, there are opportunities to make money. Old jeans have doubled in value over the past couple of decades, as fashion-conscious dressers have turned their backs on modern versions churned out identically for both supermarkets and boutiques. Levi jeans are the most collectable. A pair of Levi's Capital Es can cost up to £500 in good wearable condition. (A Levi logo – known as Capital Es – was stitched on both sides of a red tab fitted to jeans in the Fifties. In 1971 the logo lost the capitals and was rebranded simply as "Levi's".)

Old Wrangler jeans are highly sought after too, while Lee jeans also have a strong following – though a vintage pair might cost less than £100. Designer brands such as the limited Signature range of Versace in the Eighties can command prices of £150. Gucci and Jean Paul Gautier from the Eighties also sell well.

Farmer is another brand currently in vogue, with the red-and-white Sixties jeans currently changing hands for £80 or more. However, although traditional cuts are in fashion, the market for later bell-bottom jeans has yet to take off.

JEAN GENIE

The record price paid for a pair of jeans is $46,532 – more than £23,000 – paid in 2001 for a pair of 1880s Levi's. A pair of classic blue "201" Levi Strauss & Co. denims, discovered after more than a hundred years in a San Francisco gold mine, sold for £18,279 in 2008.

The history of cotton denim being used for clothing stretches back to the 17th century but it wasn't until 1873, when Levi's patented and sold riveted jeans for Nevada miners, that jeans were born.

Jeans caught the imagination of workers in the Thirties, when seen worn by cowboys in Western movies. However, they were not embraced as fashion statements until the rebellious youth of the Fifties turned their back on conservative dress with help from movie stars like James Dean and Marlon Brando.

It was also in the Fifties that modern stitching and the fitting of zippers was introduced, thus rendering them more practical as well as desirable items for the wardrobe.

Telltale signs to establish whether jeans are collectable include selvages – white seams under the inside leg. These seams were discontinued for Levi's in 1982. Position of rivet, pocket location, stitching type and colour all indicate the age.

The stitching on the inside of the turn-ups might be white, or white and red, depending on whether the denim came from the middle or at the edge of a roll – the red and white at the edge is often seen as better, harder wearing denim.

Look to see if jeans have a "care label" inside. If they do the chances are your vintage denims are nothing but a fake. The more overall colour the denim has retained, the more valuable it is.

Wash with care. Fading and tears decrease value so although the jeans may be worn it is better to save them for special – not dirty – occasions and to dry clean. The retro appearance does not look good accompanied by iron creases.

RAGS TO RICHES

Although vintage jeans can be found on internet trading sites such as eBay, specialist second-hand clothes stores may be a better starting place for the novice investor. Charity shops occasionally throw up gems.

Koi Carp

Koi is an abbreviation of *nishikigoi*, the Japanese term for "brocaded carp". This exotic fish comes in a wide variety of vibrant colours, patterns and prices to suit all pockets.

Costs can start at £20 for a six-inch koi, going up to more than £2000 for a fine three-footer. Koi can even change hands for half a million pounds. The British record is £100,000 for "Jessica Rose", 2006 winner of the All-Japan Koi Show.

It is rare, but you can make money – it just requires great skill and lots of luck to develop a prize winner that others will want for beauty or breeding. A £50 fish can grow to be worth more than £1000 in five years (with some dollops of good fortune).

However, for every winner there are likely to be several losers – and the cost of looking after koi properly tends to eat into any profits that you are likely to make.

Size counts and a healthy fish can grow to four feet in length. Investors tend to go for broad, blunt-nosed heads that taper to a thick well-muscled tail. The skin should be even textured and smooth.

There are 13 basic varieties of koi from which to choose, with the Kohaku being the most popular. These are white with red – "beni" – patterns on head and body; the most collectable having deep uniform shading. Find one with a Japanese flag "sun" on the forehead and you may have a great investment.

Breeding is best kept to the experts and top quality koi are rarely picked up at bargain prices because traders realise the values of the fish may grow, in fact, as they grow.

Koi generally survive for about thirty or forty years but can live for 100 years or even longer. A young koi might grow by up to 18 inches in four years.

LIVING JEWEL

Enthusiasts believe koi are living jewels. It is a lifestyle choice to keep koi and not an easy way to make money. If you cannot treat them as very demanding pets do not bother!

Expenses begin with a pool. Koi need plenty of space in which to swim, with a pool typically at least six feet deep and with 50 square feet to keep them trim. A basic pond can be installed for £2000, but once you have finished with all the necessary filtering and possible heating equipment the bill can rise to £5000.

Food is also a major cost. A 15kg bag of quality pellet food is £100 and a dozen koi might guzzle their way through this in a month. To help the skin glow, the Japanese use mud baths. Clay conditioner in Britain can cost £80 for a 5kg bag.

Heating is not essential but koi in winter may disappear to the bottom of the pond and refuse to eat – so £30 a week spent on keeping them warm may also be money well spent.

Start small with £20 fish that may not win any prizes but give you a couple of years to learn the skills to properly look after koi. This is especially prudent given that they are hard to insure and worthless when dead. The British Koi Keepers' Society offers details of local clubs that can provide guidance and support. There is a deadly disease, the Koi Herpes Virus (KHV), that has wiped out many ponds; purchase advice is therefore essential.

The majority of fish are sourced from Japan where koi breeding began more than 300 years ago, and local experts should be able to provide a full account of their origins.

GOING FISHING

Read up before taking the plunge. Try *How to Keep Koi: An Essential Guide*, by David Twigg. The British Koi Keepers' Society has details of local groups (www.bkks.co.uk). See also *Koi Carp Magazine* (www.nishikigoi.co.uk); and *Koi Magazine* (www.koimag.co.uk).

Lego

Building a fortune can be child's play with Lego. The Danish plastic bricks have come a long way since first put together in 1949, and what was once old toy clutter can now fetch hundreds of pounds as an adventurous investment. Until a few years ago you could pick up second-hand Lego at car boot sales for next to nothing – but investors are waking up to the market and great deals are increasingly rare.

The limited editions or the very oldest sets are the best investments. For modern Lego, figurines and pricey limited editions tend to be the most collectable. For example, an Airport Shuttle Monorail that cost £100 in 1990 may now be worth £1000.

The oldest Lego sets were often sold in wooden boxes with sliding lids, and can now fetch more than £300. The early bricks were hollow inside, unlike the stud-and-tube style plastic building blocks that were introduced in 1958. The Lego bricks initially only came in red and white and were matt cellulose. A tougher ABS plastic Lego came out in 1963.

Founder Ole Kirk Christiansen started the firm in 1932 selling stepladders, ironing boards and wooden toys. He came up with the Lego name by combining the two Danish words *leg* and *gotd* – meaning "play well". This also hit upon the nice symmetry that "lego" can be translated as "I put together" in Latin.

But it wasn't until 1947 that Lego snapped up Denmark's first injection-moulding machine and began to make plastic toys. In 1949, inspired by English round-

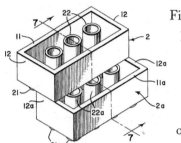

studded plastic building blocks designed by Hilary "Harry" Fisher Page, Lego started producing Automatic Binding Bricks.

Modern Lego has the logo clearly embossed on each brick dimple and is made of injection-moulded acrylonitrile butadiene styrene. Imitation bricks made by other firms are regarded as worthless junk by most investors, and even Lego's own bigger-sized Duplo bricks tend not to hold their value.

OVER-POPULATION?

There are 62 Lego bricks for every person on the planet.

The Lego market for Star Wars figurines is one of the biggest, with values at least doubling in the past five years. Among the most collectable is a Millennium Falcon that might have cost less than £100 in 2000, but which is now worth well over £500.

A 2007 Lego metallic gold C-3PO also attracted huge interest. Lego distributed 10,000 figures randomly throughout their Star Wars range, with some lucky sets that were bought for £10 soon soaring to £200 in value.

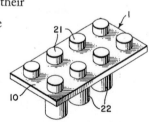

However, the ultimate Lego is worth more than its weight in gold – even though the pieces are actually made of that precious metal. These gold bricks were presented to loyal former workers at the Danish factory; and sellers can essentially name their price.

 ## BUILDING A FORTUNE

Those interested in investing in Lego should look at dedicated online Lego-trading forum Bricklink (www.bricklink.com). There is also an adult Lego club called Brickish that offers advice on collecting as well as building projects to capture the imagination – a key appeal for investors, as they are building enthusiasts as well. See The Brickish Association at www.brickish.org. Official website www.Lego.com also has details of limited editions. Visit Legoland in Windsor, Berkshire for sheer inspiration.

Luggage

The adventurous gentleman didn't travel lightly when out exploring. He would have a small army of servants to carry trunks, suitcases, hold-alls, hat boxes, cruiser bags, shoe cases, briefcases, toilet sets and clutch bags – plus the odd but essential frippery, such as a travelling cocktail set.

Weight and space were minor considerations in the era before baggage allowance and airport lost & found, but quality was a major concern. It is therefore of little surprise that ancient luggage is highly sought after. Dusty trunks and bags once seen as junk in the attic are being rediscovered as vintage treasure chests worth hundreds or even thousands of pounds.

Louis Vuitton is the benchmark for quality luggage. He set up the firm as a packing case maker in 1854 and was official trunk-maker to Empress Eugenie of France. He also arranged the carriage of expensive costumes in wooden chests for the European aristocracy.

Cases were made for specific purposes. Unusual examples include a travelling bed that folded into a trunk, made by the explorer Pierre de Brazza when he set off to the Congo in 1875. Another is an early 20th century trunk fit to hold a set of *Encyclopaedia Britannica* – now worth more than the books at up to £1500.

Vuitton revolutionised the baggage industry with flat-top trunks, canvas material (rather than leather) to render them waterproof and the addition of plenty of storage accessories. Among the most desired are Victorian wardrobe trunks, selling for £1500 as decorative items. Others include a tea chest, with cups, flasks and tray, for £500. Rarities, like pink trunks, can go for £3000.

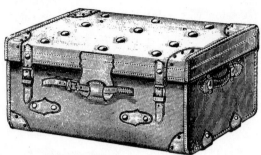

The best British luggage-makers have a reputation for being less externally flashy than their continental counterparts, saving the attention to detail for an interior that only the owner (and butler who unpacked it) could admire.

Finnigans, originally of Manchester and later Bond Street, is one of the finest. Other great names include Drew & Sons, and Asprey and Irving Brothers of Edinburgh. Typical prices for old trunks start at £500 but may rise to £1000.

The first Gladstone bags – named after the British Prime Minister and his travelling luggage – were made by J. G. Beard of Westminster. Foreign top luggage names in addition to Vuitton that still hold collectible cachet today include Cartier, Hermès, Gucci and Goyard.

PIC-NIC UP A BARGAIN

The vintage picnic hamper is particularly in demand from classic car owners. Great names that sell from £300 upwards include Coracle, Vickery, Mappin & Webb, Drew & Sons, Sirram and Barratt & Sons. Bone china accessories are typical but seek fun extras such as kettles, spirit burners, wicker-bound milk bottles and cocktail sets. Dig out a wind-up gramophone player to provide the soundtrack.

Initials are often stamped on luggage and this can make them less appealing to investors with a different name. However, if it includes labels – ideally London Savoy and Orient Express – romance grabs the heart, and eases open the wallet.

Polishing is required: old leather that reeks of quality can crumble if not looked after. The golden era for luggage was probably the period spanning the 1880s to the 1920s; after this the arrival of air travel meant bags tended to be lighter and less extravagant. Discover a honey-coloured leather weekend case from the Twenties and you have an investment that will probably never fall in value.

TRAVELLING IN STYLE

Major auction houses like Christie's and Bonhams often include vintage luggage in sales, but for real bargains check out the attic, ask elderly relatives, and go hunting at jumble and boot sales. Remember, careful polishing can turn a tatty relic into a classic investment.

Magic Tricks

Wave a wand for potentially spellbinding returns with vintage conjuring tricks. Interest in the history of illusion has sent values soaring in recent years, with cheap props once thrown away as rubbish now fetching thousands of pounds.

The golden era of conjurers began in the mid-19th century with "father of magic" Jean Eugène Robert-Houdin, from whom Harry Houdini took his name. Robert-Houdin was the first to don an evening suit and amaze guests with the "ethereal suspension" trick – levitating women. Examples of his work are hard to find, but a Robert-Houdin advertising fan used by flustered guests can now fetch as much as £3000.

The early 20th century escapologist Houdini is the most collectable of all. You won't escape with a pair of original Houdini handcuffs for less than £5000, while magician David Copperfield paid £140,000 for his "water torture cell" in 2004. This unique glass box was filled to the top with water before a bound and manacled Houdini was dramatically lowered into its depths – and had to escape.

Among the most collectable magic props are the colourful posters that were used to promote magicians' acts in the golden era of the early 20th century. One of the most collectable is Chung Ling Soo, who produced a large range of fabulous Oriental posters bearing the imprint of his exotic imagination.

His posters were used as wrapping paper for magic tricks in World War II during a paper shortage but can now fetch £12,000 to £20,000. Other collectable greats from the late 19th and early 20th century include John Nevil Maskelyne, Harry Kellar, The Great Lafayette, David Devant, Dante, Howard Thurston, Charles Carter and Horace Goldin.

CATCH THE BULLET

Famous magician Chung Ling Soo was not actually Chinese but an American called Billy Robinson who kept up his impersonation with perfect attention to detail – only speaking to reporters through interpreters, for example. He was shot dead in a botched "catch the bullet" trick in Britain in 1918. 'Oh my God. Something's happened. Lower the curtain.' These words, spoken at the fatal moment, were the first – and last – time in 19 years he ever spoke English on stage.

Magicians do not want their secrets exposed, so the most expensive part of a magical investment can often be buying how the illusion works. A 1970 book *The Magic of Robert Harbin* – of which only 500 were made before printing plates were destroyed – is now worth £700. It shows, amongst other things, how to successfully saw a woman in half.

British magician Peter Selbit invented the iconic sawing-a-lady-in-half in 1921. An original prop involved might fetch tens of thousands of pounds.

A derivative "zig-zag lady" trick created by the aforementioned Robert Harbin in the late Sixties, where the assistant wiggles different parts of her anatomy from separate boxes, is worth at least £10,000 to learn.

THE MAGIC CIRCLE

Investors hoping to use a collected prop for a trick must realise they also need a magician's skill and practice to operate it. Any budding magician can contact the Magic Circle.

There are 1600 members of the Magic Circle and applicants must be recommended by two members for an audition in which to demonstrate their illusionist's skills.

Modern props tend to be trashed after use and are rare, while the early ones were built to be more substantial and got regularly repaired and redeployed. An original prop from a Paul Daniels "chop cup" routine – using one cup and a ball – deployed in the famous Bunko Booth might fetch £500.

An unused magic set for a modern TV magician like David Nixon might cost as little as £50, while signed photos from comic legend Tommy Cooper can fetch hundreds of pounds.

INVESTMENTS OUT OF A HAT

A good place to start is to contact local magic clubs and read historic books to whet the appetite and then visit a specialist shop. Davenports Magic, and International Magic Shop, are among the best stores that sell modern tricks and offer a great place for free advice and local magic course details. Their magic kits start at just a few pounds but can cost several thousand – especially for the larger illusionary set pieces.

The Magic Circle's website is at www.themagiccircle.co.uk. Davenports Magic may be found at www.davenportsmagic.co.uk; International Magic Shop at www.internationalmagic.com. Also check out America's oldest magic shop trader Martinka (www.martinka.com).

Maps

If you do not want to get lost in the world of investments why not put money into antique maps? Prices of collectable maps and atlases have more than doubled over the past decade thanks to growing appreciation of their unique appeal.

 ## IN THE PINK

A colonial obsession with mapping was key to the adventurous expeditions that led Britain to conquer huge swathes of the world and colour it in an eye-pleasing shade of pink. Empire maps, such as the 1872 Archibald Fullerton, can sell for £600 – while a Walter Crane Imperial Federation Map costs £1500.

The blueprint for the Earth was mapped out almost 2000 years ago by Claudius Ptolemy in his *Geographia*. However, no ancient examples survive and it wasn't until 1477 in Bologna that the first copies of this charting of the classic world were discovered.

These maps were used as guides by explorer Christopher Columbus in 1492 when he made it to America – but thought he had arrived in China. This is because although the ancient maps were well detailed, and covered a quarter of the world, they had underestimated the size of the real world by about a third.

For adventurous investors, the first examples that recognise America are the most valuable of all. Martin Waldseemüller produced the first world map with the term America on it in 1507, having allegedly named the continent after explorer Amerigo Vespucci. The only surviving copy of the wall map was sold for a record-breaking $10m – though worth many millions more – to the United States Library of Congress in 2001.

In 1570, the first modern atlas was produced by Abraham Ortelius – the *Theatrum Orbis Terrarum*. It was so successful that 31 editions were produced from 1570-1612. Even today, random pages of it can be picked up or sold on for £500. A complete Ortelius atlas can fetch £200,000 – but could have been purchased for less than £10,000 in the Sixties.

One of most appealing markets is the 17th century golden age of map-making, where mythical artwork was regularly included – featuring some magnificent decorations of sea monsters, galleons and angels blowing horns.

The Dutch were particularly skilled at map-making. In the early 17th century the famous Dutch cartographer house of Blaeu was established and examples from that time typically go from £500 to £20,000. Discover a Blaeu *Le Grand Atlas, ou Cosmographie Blaviane*, in the attic and you may have a £200,000 asset.

Although world maps are among the most valuable, the early British maps are also highly collectable and can be bought for less money.

Christopher Saxton in the 1570s was the first to produce county maps in Britain, with examples typically going for £4000 to £7000. He was followed by John Speed, whose

English counties can go for £500 to £1500. From 1675 John Ogilby produced the first road maps and these prices start at £200, along with those of another great cartographer Robert Morden.

Almost all of the antique maps were originally in atlas books but were later taken out by collectors. However, nowadays maps are worth more if in an original atlas. Be careful when buying maps in a frame as it is difficult to check condition and colour quality – both these factors are key when considering investments.

Maps made before 1800 tend to have survived better than some later ones because they were produced on rag paper rather than pulp. Be wary of early reproductions that may be marketed as important originals.

GETTING YOUR BEARINGS

Excellent guides include *The Map Book*, by Peter Barber; *Antique Maps: A Collector's Guide*, by Carl Moreland and David Bannister. Dealers include The Map House of London (www.themaphouse.com).

Marbles

Marble collecting is not child's play. The earliest marbles were made more than 6000 years ago in Egypt and surviving examples are now worth at least £10,000. Romans also used stone marbles for playing games.

Glass marbles were introduced in the 15th century by European glassworkers, using "end of the day" leftover glass, for their children. However, it was not until the late 1840s that decorated glass marbles became popular. Earliest examples from the German town of Lauscha are highly collectable and can trade for £2000.

In 1870 a technique was devised to enable marbles to be made without a mark being left from the glass rod in manufacture. Victorian examples from this era typically sell for £50. At the same time, some desirable marbles known as Sulphides – glass balls with small clay figures inside – started to be produced. Basic sulphides made in the 19th century can fetch more than £100 but the most desirable examples with figures inside and coloured glass change hands for up to £2000.

It wasn't until the Americans began churning out machine-made colourful glass balls of their own in the early 20th century that the modern collectable scene was born. Schoolboy classics such as Popeyes, Peltiers and Peerless Patches fought it out in the playground with Oxbloods, Egg Yokes and Onion Skins.

Companies such as the American Alley Agate and the Christensen offshoot Akro Agate – producer of the "Aggies" – and Peltier Glass Company are among the most collectable, with their marbles changing hands from £5 all the way up to £500.

The modern "cat's eye" marbles that were mass-produced and imported from Japan from the 1950s onwards tend to be worth a few pennies rather than pounds.

SHOOTING A TOLLY

Marbles is properly played in an arena six-feet wide, on a surface three inches higher than the surrounding area, covered with sand. The idea is to knock the opponent's marble out of the ring with a skilful flick of the thumb – shooting a "Tolly" – where only the knuckle of the index finger can touch the edge of the ring. Get caught "fudging" (moving the hand forwards in a shot), or "cabbaging" (aiming from the wrong point), and you get penalised for a foul.

Quality swirl design, colours and simple eye-candy appeal are all part of the charm that dictates marble prices – on top of pedigree. Favourites such as the Akro corkscrews have up to five colour spirals. Condition is also vital: any scratch or blemish from playing will typically knock the value down by at least a half.

PLAYING MARBLES FOR MARRIAGE

The annual Good Friday British and World Championships for Marbles is held at Tinsley Green in West Sussex. The event can be traced to Elizabethan times when suitors played for the hand of a Tinsley maid. Judged equal at archery, falconry and wrestling, they had to play marbles to see who would tie the knot.

Apart from play, marble manufacturers also make artistic balls that are *just* for collecting. Makers such as Mark Matthews, Ro Purser and Chris Juedemann are skilled at creating dozens of colour swirls, known as filigrana, within their marbles, as well as beautiful internal mosaics called murrines – commanding up to £2000 a shot for each of their intricate and delicate designs.

KEEPING YOUR MARBLES

Learn the rules and meet enthusiasts through the British Marbles Board of Control (www.britishmarbles.org.uk). House of Marbles has a marble museum in Bovey Tracey, Devon, and a large online store (www.houseofmarbles.com). Books to study include *Collecting Antique Marbles: Identification and Price Guide*, by Paul Baumann.

Meccano

The decline of the British manufacturing industry is mirrored by the fall in popularity of Meccano as a toy. Invented in 1901 as Mechanics Made Easy, and containing just 16 pieces, it was renamed Meccano in 1907 after becoming a hit. The Meccano moniker was coined from an educational phrase – "Make and Know".

Sets became more complex and ambitious, and included motorised cars, cranes, transporter bridges, steam engines, World War I fighter planes, carousels and Ferris wheels. These early sets fetch hundreds of pounds with the most sought after being the Meccano No. 10 box from the firm's heydey in 1937. This can reach a price of £1500 today. Even at the time this huge set was expensive at £11 in old money – and £50 in the Seventies.

However, discover a later 1939 No. 10 set with rare accessories and you could be looking at an investment worth £4000. Any unusual extras – such as ship's funnels and compass needles – create a stir, as investors need to complete sets.

Another sought after piece from the company's Thirties heyday is Meccano Block Setting Crane, which can sell for £1250. A Fifties shop display model of Blackpool Tower sold for £2500 in 2004.

The first Mechanics Made Easy cost seven shillings and sixpence (37.5p) – half the weekly wage of the average labourer. Today they can fetch several hundred pounds at auction.

DAY-DREAMING TO A FORTUNE

Frank Hornby invented Meccano after staring out from his office as a clerk in Liverpool and admiring a crane. The 37-year-old went home and made a copy using flat pieces of metal drilled with holes, held together with nuts and bolts. He gave it to his sons, Roland, 12, and Douglas, 11. All their friends then wanted a set. So Hornby quit his job and, in 1901, patented metal toy sets – going into business with Mechanics Made Easy.

Meccano also proved a great investment of time for future engineers and scientists. Nobel prize winner for chemistry, Sir Harry Kroto, said Meccano was key in his childhood and helped him to understand molecular structures.

In 1921 the first properly engineered motorcar Meccano sets were made. The cars were driven by an electric motor, had a clutch, three-speed gearbox, suspension and brakes. These intricate, accurate designs enabled future engineers to gain an early understanding of mechanics.

Without box or original instructions – and of course, every nut, bolt, strut, cog, and axle – values plummet. Ideally the pieces should still be tied into the box. The early boxes are particularly sought after because of their fantastic image of a friendly pipe-smoking father helping his son build a Meccano set.

Meccano in Colours was introduced in 1926, with red, green and brass parts available. The colours changed five times over the next five decades so seek help from an expert dealer for authentic dating of pieces.

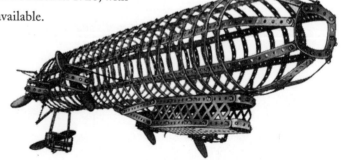

The firm was taken over in 1964, and with dwindling demand – as youngsters took to computer game joysticks rather than nuts, bolts and perforated metal strips – passed through various hands, until today, when it is owned by the Japanese firm Nikko.

Modern Meccano now even includes power tools to make life easier for children.

 MAKE AND KNOW

Start by contacting a local enthusiast group. Details and information are available from the International Society of Meccanomen at www.internationalmeccanomen.org.uk. Specialist auctioneers include Vectis (www.vectis.co.uk).

Medals

The Victoria Cross for 'most conspicuous bravery ... in the presence of the enemy' is the highest of all awards and has only been granted 1356 times since being introduced in 1856. A Victoria Cross that sold for £10,000 20 years ago and £30,000 at the start of the decade will now go for £90,000 or even more. However, as with all medals, its history hugely affects value.

The record paid is £491,567 in 2006 for a VC posthumously awarded to New Zealand-born Captain Alfred John Shout. He led a bayonet charge against heavy machine gun fire at Gallipoli in 1915 while fighting for the Australian Imperial Force. The previous record was £235,250 in 2004 for a VC awarded to WWII airman, the late Warrant Officer Norman Jackson. He crawled onto the fuselage of a blazing Lancaster bomber at 20,000ft to extinguish a fire while under attack from a German fighter. Shot down and badly injured he later escaped a prisoner of war camp.

After the Victoria Cross, the George Cross is a near equivalent civilian award 'for gallantry', as well as for great acts of bravery by military personnel *not* in the direct face of the enemy. These fetch £12,000 to £25,000 at auction.

There is also a Conspicuous Gallantry Cross – just a notch below – awarded 29 times since its inception in 1993. So far none have hit the market, but they could go for five-figure sums.

THE ORIGINS OF THE VICTORIA CROSS

The Victoria Cross medals are cast from the gunmetal of two cannons captured from the Russians at the siege of Sevastopol during the Crimean War in the 1850s. The Crimean War was the first time Queen Victoria recognised acts of ultimate valour 'in the presence of the enemy' with medals.

The historic stature of the Great War, in particular, makes related medals highly collectable. A good place to start is with local regional battalions, many of which have long been disbanded. These include specially formed "pals battalions" of friends, neighbours and work colleagues, separate from Army regiments.

A Military Medal was awarded for gallantry above and beyond the call of duty, and Great War examples can fetch between £300 and £500. Even a standard campaign medal from World War I fetches £100.

The value of a medal is heavily linked with the story of how it was awarded, though, and not just the conflict and the basic worth.

For example, a set of Military Medal awards given to Falklands War "Goose Green" veteran Lance Corporal "Bill" Bentley sold for £39,200 in 2007. The value was increased by an incredible story involving him amputating a badly injured leg of a comrade with a Swiss Army Knife to save his life, while under fire.

A standard service medal from the Crimean War between 1853 and 1856 might fetch £250 but a medal for those involved in the Charge of the Light Brigade may fetch as much as £10,000.

The role of movies also has a huge impact on values. The Zulu War service medal of 1879 is worth £400. However, find one awarded to a figure who featured in the 1964 film of the famous British defence of Rorke's Drift, and it could be worth £30,000. The service medal for Lieutenant Gonville Bromhead, played by Sir Michael Caine in the film, would fetch double this amount.

BRAVE THE MARKET

Short of signing up with the armed forces tomorrow, start with the medal collectors' bible *Collecting Medals and Decorations*, by Alec Purves. Industry magazine *Medal News* provides information and details of specialist medal collectors and reputable traders.

Mobile Phones

T he revenge of the yuppie has arrived in the shape of the vintage brick-sized mobile phone. A few years ago you couldn't give away these handsets, but now collectors pay hundreds of pounds for the iconic Eighties fashion accessory.

The granddaddy of the mobile is the Motorola DynaTAC 8000x, which was launched in 1983. This impressive big beast looks more like a doorstep than a brick and cost a whopping £1200 when new and boasted a one-hour talk time. As an historic artefact you can now pay £600 for a well looked after example.

The Motorola model launched just before the DynaTAC 8000x was the Traveller, lugged around in a heavy briefcase. But even without the same mobile cachet, it is still worth more than £100.

However, in 1987 Motorola brought out its 8500x model, which is perhaps is the most iconic brick handset of all, made famous by wannabe Yuppie Del Boy in the TV comedy *Only Fools and Horses*. It was followed up by the very first flip-top, the Motorola MicroTAC in 1989. To look the part it had a fake antenna and microphone hole. The very earliest ones had red LED displays and sell for up £150.

The early models were analogue so cannot accept SIM cards and be used today – they are more collectable items for interior decoration, with limited practical use such as trendy bookends.

However, if you want an old handset as a collectable investment you should still look out for one with an original box and extras such as leather holding case and extra rechargeable batteries.

Later mobile phones also have investment appeal. A design class is the limited edition walnut effect Nokia 2110, favoured by Jaguar-driving company directors in the Nineties. These handsets were thrown away as junk a couple of years ago but now command prices of up to £100.

BEAM ME UP

The late Nineties Motorola StarTAC phone was modelled on communicators used in the Sixties Sci-Fi TV series *Star Trek*. It was the first mini-mobile with flip-top and was a benchmark for future models – it also accepts modern SIM cards. Examples go for £50, as with sibling MicroTAC, but prices are rising.

Luxury mobiles that are made to exclusive designs and only produced in limited numbers can also offer investment potential – possibly as artistic pieces of jewellery and not just iconic handsets. These include the ultra-slim 2004 Japanese Talby mobile designed by Australian Marc Newson, which can cost up to £1000 a handset as a design piece, and is displayed in London's Design Museum.

The super-rich mobile of choice is the Vertu range, available new for as much as £20,000, with a platinum-finished handset with sapphire crystal face and jewelled bearings under each key.

DON'T BIN THE PHONE

The vast majority of mobile phones will never amount to being much more than rubbish as an investment but should still never just be thrown away. Charities such as Oxfam, the Guide Dogs for the Blind Association, ActionAid, the War Memorials Trust and Hearing Dogs For Deaf People can recycle the handsets.

The market for buying old mobiles is fragmented but eBay offers a good trading place. Specialist dealers may also help. These include www.vintagemobilephones.com and www.retrobrick.com.

Money

Look after the pennies and the pounds will look after themselves. A worthy but dull proverb for those seeking extraordinary investments – unless it is being stashed away in rare old cash. One Penny is typically worth, well pennies, but find one of only a dozen struck in 1933 and you have a £30,000 discovery. Only one was struck in 1954 and it sold for £24,000 more than 15 years ago.

Meanwhile, ancient coins dating as far back as Roman times can provide incredibly good value, enabling you to invest in a fascinating piece of history for just a few pounds.

However, a numismatist, or coin collector, should not be confused with an investor who focuses only on top quality examples that are extremely rare (and not necessarily the most eye-catching). His tastes are usually more catholic, and concerned more with aesthetics or history.

The most collectable coins have enjoyed bumper returns over the past 15 years, enjoying growth in value averaging about 10% per annum.

The most historically valuable coin in Britain is thought to be a 9th century gold piece depicting Coenwulf, the ruler of the Anglo-Saxon kingdom of Mercia. It was discovered by a treasure-hunter near Bedford in 2001 and snapped up by the British Museum for £357,832.

However, the record *price* for a coin goes to an Edward III Gold Double Florin – known as a Double Leopard – dating from 1344. It was bought for £460,000 in 2006 as one of only three thought to exist.

Americans are willing to pay even more for their prize collectable cash. In 1913 the US mint produced millions of buffalo-head five-cent pieces but only a handful of Liberty-head nickels. These rare Liberty headed 1913 coins can sell for £800,000.

Ancient coins were often tampered with and bits casually chipped off to melt down and make other money. Later British coins bear the important motto *DECUS ET TUTAMEN* – Ornament and Safeguard – and tend to be less susceptible to forgeries.

Coin collectors are particularly picky and go for examples in fabulous condition; uncirculated is great but there is an even more perfect mint state known as "Fleur de coin". A scarce Old Penny from 1869 might fetch a fiver if recovered from an old jam jar, but if it was never circulated could go for more than £500.

 BANKING ON NOTES

In the late 18th century, private banks issued their own notes separate from the Bank of England currency. These "town notes" attract specialist interest and can fetch thousands. The highest price paid for a £1 note is £55,000 handed over for a 1797 example. An 18th century £100 note can change hands for as much as £40,000. As a rule of thumb, the higher denominations usually fetch more.

Do not be tempted to surreptitiously improve the value of any collectable change you have. If you polish a coin in a natural state you can knock up to a third off the value.

Limited edition coins or special editions are dismissed by most serious numismatists as fairly worthless. The fact that so many people tuck them away for safekeeping only lowers the chance of investment returns.

COINING IT IN

A great first coin is the magnificent George III cartwheel penny of 1797. These 1.5 diameter coins were minted to show off new steam-driven coin presses and weighed an ounce. They can be picked up on the open market for as little as £20.

Bone up on the subject with books. Essential tomes include *British Coins Market Values,* by various authors depending on the year, and *Collectors' Coins GB* and *Collectors' Banknotes* by Christopher Henry Perkins. Full details of dealers are available from the Coin Dealers Directory, www.numis.co.uk; the British Numismatic Trade Association, www.bnta.net and industry magazine *Coin News.*

Monopoly

The hardship of jail or heartbreak of bankruptcy at the hands of a ruthless family member may have its plus side – if the arena is an ancient Monopoly board. Since the game started being produced by Parker Brothers in 1935, more than 200m Monopoly boards have been sold worldwide, making it the most popular game in history.

The first Monopoly set was made by unemployed engineer Charles Darrow and was snapped up for £45,000 more than 15 years ago by business magazine *Forbes*. Pre-war editions fetch more than £100 if in tip-top condition. Even the black-box covered editions, made up to the Sixties, fetch more than £50 a piece. However, later "limited editions" are rarely worth much.

The similar games that pre-date Monopoly are the most valuable of all. The Landlord's Game, invented by Virginian Quaker Lizzie Magie in 1903, is widely regarded as the forefather of Monopoly – though it was designed as an aid to understanding taxes, rather than financially crushing all your foes. Copies of the Landlord's Game have fetched more than £50,000 at auction.

Another early game, Bulls and Bears, invented like Monopoly by Darrow, is worth at least £20,000. A British rental board game similar to Monopoly called Brer Fox and Brer Rabbit can also fetch five-figure sums.

These really old games are hand-made and printed on cloth.

GREAT TRAIN ROBBERS

There was a total of $15,140 of play money in the original Monopoly. The Great Train Robbery gang of 1963 stole £2.6m in the biggest ever heist in Britain and substituted real cash for the board game's funny money while hiding out. It landed them in jail without passing Go, as fingerprints were found on a set.

Until the explosion of board games in the 20th century, when games became focused on family entertainment, the options were fairly limited and tended to be educational and based on snakes and ladders-type rules.

It is this nostalgia among parents and grandparents eager to get youngsters to share in the joys they experienced when they were growing up that fuels the present-day investment market. Games linked into intellectual property still known today also tend to do best.

Find *The Archers* Board Game by Chad Valley in the attic and a loyal love for the BBC radio series means it should fetch £100 – even though it wasn't a great hit when it came out in the Sixties. Likewise, an early Seventies pop game fronted by Tony Blackburn called Chart Buster could be picked up for £5 just over a decade ago but now – post-reality TV excursions, and with wistful longing for the old Top of the Pops rising – it fetches £150.

Star Wars collectable games, such as the 1977 Adventures of R2-D2, can still be picked up for about £12, but kept in near-mint condition – and not played with – and such investments will rarely lose value.

Blue-chip classics such as an early 20th century The Popular Game of Railway Race will always command prices of at least £50 just for the nostalgic bright artwork of the cover.

Waddingtons' attempt to cash in on the success of Monopoly with a horse racing Totopoly in the late Thirties was a flop – but surviving examples now trade for £70.

 ## PASSING GO

Dust down the Monopoly board and invite friends round; if still talking at the end of the night pass Go, and collect a pat on the back. Check out the Association of Game & Puzzle Collectors at www.agpc.org. Traders include Alvin's Vintage Games (www.vintage-games.co.uk).

Moon Rock

Moon rock-hunters and Mars explorers have enjoyed staggering prices for their extraterrestrial treasures, with exceptional pieces selling for as much as £40,000 a gram.

However, prices vary hugely and it requires a rather expert eye to sort through all the earth-dwelling rubble to find valuable bits of asteroids, old stars, other planets, dirty chunks of comet and the Moon.

The vast majority of meteorite fragments are bits of rock and metal broken off from collisions in the asteroid belt between Mars and Jupiter, taking 100m years to get to Earth. Rock from Mars and the Moon comes from direct hits by asteroids or large meteorites.

The debris comes in all shapes and sizes, from tiny specs that can only be viewed under a microscope to huge boulders that would not even fit through the door.

Most meteorites are silicon or carbon-based rocks. However, there are also many metal-based meteorites that contain iron and nickel that should be kept in dry storage rather than allowed to rust on the mantelpiece.

Mars and the Moon are amongst the most attractive investments, and their rocks typically sell for up to £2000 a gram, though particularly rare specimens have sold for £40,000 a gram.

An interesting looking standard meteorite rock weighing 2kg can fetch £1200 while a standard 1kg boulder the size of a cricket ball might cost £250. Standard meteorites the size of a golf ball can be picked up for less than £100.

OLDER THAN EARTH

Meteorites can be 4.6 billion years old, providing a chance to study the original dust from which our Solar System was formed – before the dawn of our own creation. Our own sun and earth were created about 4.5 billion years ago.

A tiny fragment of a shooting star can be picked up for less than a fiver.

Prices rise if the rock falls at an auspicious time and place. For example, bits of the Barwell meteorite, which fell on the Leicestershire village of that name on Christmas Eve 1965, can cost £200 for a 2.5g slither the size of a fingernail. When it first fell to earth the Natural History Museum was offering 'seven and sixpence an ounce' (about 10p for 30 grams).

A less auspicious but much heavier 25g fragment of the Gibeon meteorite, which landed in the Namibian desert of Africa in 1836, is far more affordable at just £30.

PENNIES FROM HEAVEN

Enthusiasts can track down a meteorite through a specialist trader who can provide a scientific identity from the Nomenclature Committee of the Meteoritical Society. All meteorites should be catalogued, detailing their make-up, plus where and when they fell. The *Catalogue of Meteorites* by the National History Museum is the industry's definitive read, listing more than 22,500 authenticated findings.

Investors should try and get hold of the main mass of a meteorite if possible, as other fragments and sliced off sections are less valuable. Anyone who stumbles across what they believe to be a piece of meteorite – which looks like slag metal – can contact a trader or the Natural History Museum for verification.

Rocks pocketed by astronauts or space probes are not legally available.

ROCK ON

Contact The National History Museum's mineralogy department via their website at www.nhm.ac.uk/research-curation/departments/mineralogy, or The Meteoritical Society (www.meteoriticalsociety.org). Traders include Fernlea Meteorites at www.meteorites.uk.com.

Movie Props

ovie memorabilia has become big business in recent years, with film set props that were once just thrown away now selling for hundreds or even thousands of pounds.

Science fiction tends to hold some of the strongest appeal thanks to a die-hard fan base and demand that does not seem to diminish over time, with movies such as *Star Wars*, *Star Trek* and *Blade Runner* always in fashion. Find a 1977 Storm Trooper helmet and you have a £15,000 investment; while a miniature building from *Blade Runner* sold for £8795 in recent years. A decade ago the items would probably have sold for less than a third of these prices. And Star Trek fans have boldly gone where no investors have dared to go before – with a record-breaking £285,000 handed over for a miniature movie prop Starship Enterprise in 2006.

Many early props, such as plastic prosthetics, have disintegrated. This adds value to the survivors, but later ones can also be valuable as so few pieces hit the open market. *Lord of the Rings* hobbit feet sell for £2000, while the tankards that they drank from can fetch £1000. Sir Ian McKellen has kept Gandalf's staff as a memento.

BE A COUCH POTATO

Authenticity is everything, yet the market is littered with replicas and fakes. It is essential to do your homework and find out exactly how the original was made. Reputable dealers and proof of provenance is vital, but the best research will involve you sitting down to study the film footage yourself with a gimlet eye.

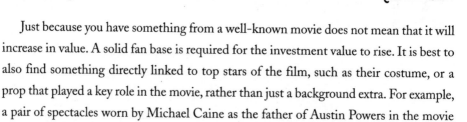

Just because you have something from a well-known movie does not mean that it will increase in value. A solid fan base is required for the investment value to rise. It is best to also find something directly linked to top stars of the film, such as their costume, or a prop that played a key role in the movie, rather than just a background extra. For example, a pair of spectacles worn by Michael Caine as the father of Austin Powers in the movie *Goldmember* sells for £1000 – while those worn by Mike Myers just in the opening credits go for £400. They had a smaller role on a comparatively lesser star.

There are certain iconic moments, movies and themes that never go out of style. *Gone With the Wind* is a classic example and anything related is priceless – with sellers able to name their own price. Others include *Casablanca*, *The Wizard of Oz* and any time Marilyn Monroe appeared on screen.

GET INTO THE MOVIES

Getting your hands on authentic pieces can require guile as these days those in the movie industry realise their increasing value and often take the rich pickings home for themselves.

Trawl through specialist shops, auctioneers and find yourself around backstage haunts if you want to bag a bargain. Building up contacts with the crews of film production is all part of the Hollywood game.

Movie props should not be confused with merchandising. Although early pieces can soar in value most "limited edition" merchandise is a marketing gimmick and a bad investment.

For details of reputable film prop auctioneers and dealers visit the website www.moviepropsassociation.org. A useful American contact is www.profilesinhistory.com while prop traders in Britain include the London-based outfit www.propstore.com.

New Art

Getting in on the ground floor by investing before a great artist has been discovered can be fantastic fun, even if the odds of success are extremely slim. If you love the art, it'll bring you priceless pleasure whatever the outcome.

One of the best places to pick up original art for a few pounds is at the end of degree Art College sales, held in the early summer every year at the start of many an artist's career.

Top colleges include the Royal College of Art in Kensington, west London, where David Hockney and Tracey Emin studied, and the Central Saint Martins College of Art and Design in central London.

Damien Hirst graduated from Goldsmiths University of London in 1988 and within two years was discovered by Charles Saatchi. In 1993 Saatchi bought a Hirst pickled shark for £50,000 – selling it for $10m 15 years later.

Another place to look for art purchases are regular local art fairs, which are often advertised in arts magazines. Outfits such as the Affordable Art Fair regularly hold sales in London, offering relatively cheap original paintings – from £50 to £3000.

Investors should be aware that luck as well as skill is required to discover a winner. Before buying, an appreciation and understanding is vital – and this means fully exploring what kind of art you love. What you love is what you should buy.

Learn about the work of artists you are considering, their backgrounds and varying styles, plus how much previous pieces have sold for, and where. Reading books, visiting public galleries and seeking advice is all part of this process.

Brave the trendy art gallery cliques of London, including Cork Street, to get advice and learn about trends. If possible, try and get invited to opening nights for exhibitions. Be aware that the best stuff often gets snapped up before the sales catalogue hits the doormat. Galleries can grab half the price in commission.

Auction houses can also throw up gems. Attending an auction without bidding is free, and a great way to learn – with outfits like Christie's, Bonhams and Sotheby's having experts that can give valuable advice for nothing.

Most art investors buy paintings for the long-term, typically more than 10 years, but prices can move rapidly in the market, requiring an ever-watchful eye. Investors should also be aware that when they sell the art they may be subject to capital gains tax, kicking in at gains above £9600 for the current tax year (09/10), and changing over time.

ART FOR ART'S SAKE?

When buying art, do not do it primarily for investment reasons but look upon it as something you love – if it rises in value then this is a bonus. Display your art proudly in a prominent place in the home – one of the great appeals of the investment is that it also doubles up as a fantastic piece of home decoration.

Follow up at the Royal College of Art (www.rca.ac.uk); Central Saint Martins College of Art and Design (www.csm.arts.ac.uk); and the Affordable Art Fair (www.affordableartfair.com). Among the publications that keep an eye on the market are *Apollo – The International Magazine for Collectors* (www.apollo-magazine.com), while the magazine *Galleries* lists details of art openings and sales (www.galleries.co.uk).

Old Toilets

Victorian toilets have more than quadrupled in value over the past decade thanks to a surge in demand for authentic bathroom fittings. A pan from the late 19th century that until recently went for a couple of hundred pounds can now fetch £1000. If you throw in a water cistern and original wooden seat, the price can double to £2000.

And if the pottery is decorated with fine prints, such as flowers, values can be pushed up past £4000 because of their extreme rarity.

Few people wish to buy toilets as a collector – most want them for personal use. This means the pan must be in excellent condition. A cracked pan is an attractive £100 plant pot rather than a useful investment worth over £1000.

The cistern-driven toilet is the most sought after as it can be plumbed into modern bathroom fittings that began to be manufactured on a large scale from the 1880s. The top investments tend to be the desirable historic brands, such as Twyfords, Royal Doulton, Jennings and Crapper.

The best place to find bargains is at a reclamation yard. But having to compete with keen-eyed speculators and antique dealers means that digging out a genuine toilet gem requires shrewd detective work – and luck. Dust them down and turn them over and look for the telltale cracks that will render them worthless.

The grandfather of all lavatories is the Sir John Harington toilet of 1594. Only two models were made, one for its maker and the other for his godmother, Queen Elizabeth I.

Although these original "John" toilets had flushing mechanisms, they were emptied once a week, so were little more than a glorified cesspit box. Neither is believed to have survived. As the most sought after of loos, they would be priceless.

SPEND A PENNY

The term "loo" is thought to be French in origin, dating back to the 18th century when ladies carried a portable commode or bordalou. The name derives from the phrase "gardez l'eau" or "watch out for the water" – a warning cry, voiced when cleaning contraptions out, that was well worth heeding. "Spend a penny" derives from charges for the first public toilets levied when first introduced more than 150 years ago.

Thomas Crapper had nothing to do with the slang term for using the toilet. This was an ancient English word that died out in the home country but took hold in America after the first settlers took the indelicate phrase with them – it only became commonly used again when re-imported during the 20th century.

Crapper made "thunder box" toilets in the 18th century that were not ceramic thrones but often made of metal and installed within wood-panelled closets. The Rolls Royce of the toilet world was the Bramah closet, patented in 1778, and still in pride of place at the Palace of Westminster. It has a complex set of gears to effectively evacuate its contents.

As the old thunder boxes are not often practical to use in modern bathrooms, their value may not increase so greatly over time, unless someone famous has used them. However, they can still fetch between £1000 and £2000 a piece.

 ## GOING BOG STANDARD

For a history of the lavatory check out *Privies and Water Closets* by David Eveleigh. Another guide is *Thunder, Flush and Thomas Crapper: An Encycloopedia* by Adam Hart-Davis. House sales often throw up unusual items such as vintage loos. Check out the small adds for local auction houses. Auctioneers that have sold old loos in the past include J. R. Hopper & Co (www.jrhopper.com) and Marilyn Swain Auctioneers (www.marilynswainauctions.co.uk). Internet site eBay regularly lists vintage toilets. Get inspired by Thomas Crapper & Co (www.thomas-crapper.com); Antique Bathrooms (www.antiquebaths.com).

Orchids

ORCHID HUNTERS

'When a man falls in love with orchids, he'll do anything to possess the one he wants. It's like chasing a green-eyed woman or taking cocaine … it's a sort of madness.'

From the Preface to *The Orchid Hunters*, by Norman MacDonald, 1939.

The allure of the orchid has maddened men into abandoning the comfort of their homes and families to go on life-threatening adventures across unexplored mountains and dangerous jungles for a single flower.

The mythical appeal comes from its symbolic relation to the erotic parts of a woman. Having been associated with virility since Greek times it is believed to hold aphrodisiac qualities and is still used in love potions today.

Yet it wasn't until the 18th century that collecting orchids became established among horticulturalists. By the 19th century orchids were in such demand that auctions were seeing prices paid for a single plant soar to £500 or more.

In 1906 the record price of $6000 was paid for an orchid. It played a major role in both funding as well as navigating expeditions during the Victorian and Edwardian era.

Orchids are grown all over the world but thrive best in isolated tropical or mountain regions rarely troubled by man – Colombia, Papua New Guinea, Tibet and Borneo still attract flower adventurers. This is where new exotic breeds are often found, which command thousands of pounds in bounty reward.

Early books on orchids are also highly sought after. A rare 19th century guide *Orchidaceae of Mexico and Guatemala* by English botanist James Bateman can fetch £300.

Orchids are the largest plant family, with more than 28,000 different breeds and 110,000 variations of hybrids. They go from the tiny thimble-sized Mystacidium up to the Triffid-challenging heights of Renanthera storei, standing 20 feet tall.

The orchid family tree fits into four main classes, three of which are air plants. The most common are Epiphytes, which grow on trees. Then there are Lithophytes, which grow on rocks, and finally the Saprophytes that prefer decaying vegetation. The fourth class, Terrestrials, like soil.

 VANILLA FLAVOUR

The vanilla plant whose magic ingredient is used for flavouring is an orchid. It was discovered by ancient Aztecs in Mexico and introduced to English gardens in 1739. Vanilla is credited for spawning the huge collectable appeal of orchids in horticulture – as well as a love for ice cream. Orchids do not come in other flavours.

The wide range of fantastic exotic flowers are as varied as they are many – from sexy and flamboyant blooms to spotted and mottled specimens that seem more reptile than plant.

Growing orchids requires more than green-fingered skill – water, light, air and a suitable fertiliser. Soil is an optional extra that most orchids do not require.

Tender attentive care is essential, including occasional re-potting, as fragile orchids have a habit of dying when you turn your back. Some experts believe that part of this therapy should also include singing and talking to the plant.

Those that come from the tropics have to be particularly well cared for in glasshouses. During the Victorian era orchids were often placed in stove houses to recreate the hot and humid conditions – only precipitating an untimely death. It takes great skill to get heat and air flow balance just right.

 GREEN FINGERED ADVICE

Orchid growers and adventurers can seek help and advice from the Orchid Society of Great Britain (www.orchid-society-gb.org.uk). The Royal Horticultural Society, www.rhs.org.uk, is also a great source of information and holds the International Orchid Register. Look for enthusiasts at local horticultural clubs.

Pedigree Pigs

Where there's muck there's brass – if pedigree pigs are wallowing in it. A wave of interest in high-class pork is creating a boom in demand for rare pigs. The value of some ancient species has been more than doubling over the past decade, as a soaring appetite for gourmet pork bangers has hit the meat market.

There are 13 indigenous British breeds of pig from which to choose.

Among the most valuable is the £1000 woolly Mangalitza, a crossbreed from a now extinct species, while the most rare is the Middle White, of which only about 200 exist – that's even less than the Siberian Tiger.

Other breeds include Old Spots, the classic-looking Tamworth, Oxford Sandy and Black, the Large White "Cornish", striped British Saddleback, British Landrace and the Welsh.

The value comes from increased demand for exclusive pork – more bangers, so to speak, for your bucks. A full-grown 70kg pig can be turned into 45kg of sausage meat: not a bad investment if you consider pedigree pig sausages can fetch £10 a kilogram.

Not only will you hopefully get good money for your meat, but the price of the pigs might rise as well. For example, Berkshire weaners – young pigs – that could be picked up for £20 a decade ago, now typically fetch £60.

While if you tap into the exotic Japanese export market, a pedigree sow picked up for £250 can be sold as a £1500 luxury breeder rather than rashers of bacon – after just 18 months of skilled pampering.

SWEATING LIKE A PIG

Pigs may have a reputation for being undiscerning eaters but, although less fussy than most, they actually have a more sophisticated palate than us. The typical pig has about 15,000 taste buds – more than any other mammal, including humans. And they don't actually sweat, which is why they wallow in mud.

Anyone with at least half-an-acre can start rearing rare breeds, with two usually being better than one to avoid loneliness. A basic sty can be built from a dozen straw bails costing £100 or a metal arc for £250.

A pig may get through 25kg of feed a month at a cost of a tenner. Pigs are typically slaughtered at 24 weeks with abattoir and butchery costs £25 and £50 respectively.

Don't get sentimental. If you feel uncomfortable about turning a Babe-style pet into rashers of bacon, pork chops or bangers, perhaps pig breeding isn't for you. (However, the food on your plate *will* taste great.)

Also, work out how you will sell the pork. It is worth contacting local traders to ensure that there is a ready nearby market to avoid making a pig's ear of your finances.

Making money is dirty work. It involves going out in all kinds of weather day and night, sacrificing holidays, turning lawns into mud baths and living close to the smells of nature.

And if you go in for breeding, you can suddenly find 20 vulnerable piglets on your hands.

 ## PIGS IN CLOVER

The British Pig Association offers full details of breeds and how to get an authentic pedigree as well as contact details for pig-breeding clubs and markets. Visit website www.britishpigs.org.

Penny Farthings

T he daredevil thrills of a Penny Farthing should be top of the list for any gentleman or lady adventurer. Its invention in 1870 by James Starley marked the official arrival of cycling as a sport. Cycling on a Penny Farthing, though, was not a leisurely pursuit but life-threatening fun.

It earned the inappropriate nickname "the Ordinary" after 1879, when the first successful chain-driven rear wheel Lawson Bicyclette – the Crocodile – was introduced. The later machines were similar to modern bikes and were known as safety bicycles. Within 15 years of invention the Farthing was obsolete.

It rusted away as novelty junk for more than a century and could be picked up as an eccentric death trap for just a few pounds in the Seventies. However, modern enthusiasts have rediscovered the exhilarating ride and as a glorious piece of Victorian history a good Penny Farthing can fetch £5000 to £10,000.

 ## COMING A CROPPER

The term "come a cropper" derives from when Penny Farthing cyclists encountered a stone or small hole. The phrase was coined to describe the head-over-heels accident which inevitably followed – with the bike doing a cartwheel and catapulting riders right over the handlebars. The bicycle was compared in this to a horse, whose rear was (and is) referred to as a croup.

A £1000 investment for a good condition classic Rudge a couple of decades ago might now be worth £5000. With cycling enthusiasm booming, interest in this pivotal part of two-wheel history means values are unlikely to fall.

Other British manufacturers with pedigree include Hillman, Herbert & Cooper and Singer – which turned skills at pedal-driven sewing machines to bikes. The Singer Xtraordinary is a highly collectable design for utilising a treadle drive.

Although the majority of these bikes were built in Britain, the Americans made their own high wheel equivalents that are often even more sought after. By the 1880s they had introduced a few modern extras like braking mechanisms, plus derivations, such as the American Star Machine, where the small wheel was at the front. Perhaps the most collectable today is the American Eagle, which has a leather clutch mechanism with levers and ratchets that had three gears – these unusual bicycles can fetch £10,000.

The larger the diameter of the front-driving wheel, the faster the bicycle can go: only the length of your leg constrains the size. This led to front wheel diameters as much as 60 inches wide, with bikes more than five feet high and able to travel at 30mph. For bike control and comfort the saddle was above the wheel.

Provenance is key to investing in these ancient vintage bikes, as few have stood the test of time without major repairs. The best rides tend to be original models of wrought iron. They also enjoyed use of ball bearings and solid rubber tyres.

The craftsmanship used in making old Penny Farthings has been lost. The first part of inspection is to try and pick it up – be suspicious if it is too heavy. Rub against the backbone to see if it has joins, indicating a repaired or new bike.

GET ON YOUR BIKE

Only a real bicycle enthusiast should get involved – it is not a punt for those of a nervous disposition with a fear of heights. Budget not just for a bike, but also maintenance costs and a step ladder. Contact a local enthusiast's group through the Veteran Cycle Club at www.v-cc.org.uk for guidance on finding a suitable bike.

Pinball

Pinball machines can provide a wizard opportunity for flipping, nudging and rolling your way into money. In the past decade collectable classics have more than doubled in value thanks to growing demand from fans keen to save them from oblivion. With the manufacturing of modern machines killed off by computer games, prices have continued to rise as vintage equipment becomes scarce while demand among players remains strong.

The best-selling pinball machine of all time is the Addams Family, made by Midway in 1992. Despite 20,000 of the pinball games being sold, a well-looked after example has risen in value from £1000 to £2500 or more over the past decade. Another great modern classic is Attack From Mars, though this can easily cost more than £3000 because of its huge appeal.

Other top games include 1998 pinball game Cactus Canyon, of which Bally Williams made only 923 before it pulled the plug. This can sell £3000 but cost £1500 five years ago. Another is Medieval Madness, a Pythonesque-game made in 1997, which has doubled in value to £2500 since it went out of production just over a decade ago.

Although machines can be picked up for just a few hundred pounds, if you pay £1000 or more then you should get a whole lot more fun and pinball equipment for your money.

Condition is key, and a bargain purchase in need of restoration can be a costly mistake. Pinball machines are similar to classic cars in that they need to be well looked after to maintain or grow in value. They are prone to breaking down due to wearing parts, such as rubber, and dirt often gets inside equipment so regular maintenance should be in the budget.

Engineers typically charge a minimum call-out of £50 but investors willing to roll up their sleeves can save themselves extra money by learning how to do basic repairs themselves. Repair advice, spare parts and buying help is available from dealers and enthusiast groups.

The history of pinball is a long and fascinating one but the modern solid-state games with circuit boards and digital displays tend to be the best ones on which to play. The very first solid-state games were introduced in 1977 but soon after the video game boom of the 1980s sounded the death knell for many pinball machines.

Pinball originates from the French 18th century game of Bagatelle. British inventor Montague Redgrave is acknowledged as making the first pinball machine in 1869 out of his factory in Cincinnati, Ohio, using a coiled spring and plunger instead of a cue.

In 1931 David Gottlieb introduced the coin-operated Baffle Ball, which was a five-balls-for-a-penny game that proved a hit in drugstores and bars across America. Other classics followed, including Ballyhoo and Contact. But it was Gottlieb's Humpty Dumpty in 1947 with its player-controlled flippers that provided the skill factor loved by pinball fans today.

Although early games are a valuable piece of history they fail to attract much interest among British investors and can be picked up for as little as £250.

FOR AMUSEMENT ONLY

The American Supreme Court of California admitted that pinball was not just a game of luck in 1974. A requirement for a gambling license was lifted and the "For Amusement Only" logo was then attached.

There is no use investing in pinball machines unless you love the game. Get down the arcade and develop those skills. Tips include reading the instructions on the console carefully to boost scores and developing nudge techniques to keep those balls up for longer.

BECOMING A PINBALL WIZARD

Visit UK Pinball Group at games.groups.yahoo.com/group/ukpinball and Pinball News at www.pinballnews.com. Traders include Pinball UK at www.pinballuk.co.uk; and The Pinball Heaven at www.pinballheaven.co.uk.

Playing Cards

Investors seeking a winning deal should consider playing cards. The most collectable decks have soared in value in recent years with packs once shuffled for pennies now changing hands for hundreds or even thousands of pounds.

Their origin is a mystery but the first reference was made in the 14th century when playing cards were banned in the Italian city of Florence for causing drunkenness and fighting.

Originally hand-painted cards, they could only be afforded by the very rich. However, the invention of the woodblock printing presses helped them gain widespread appeal from the 16th century.

They swiftly took over from dice as the favoured gambling game, with pontoon and poker becoming one of the main attractions – after alcohol – in gin houses and gaming clubs.

The English government, keen to stamp out gambling (and seeking new ways to make money) introduced playing card taxes, first in 1588 and 1628, but more widely from 1711. At the tax height in the early 1800s, a farthing (0.25p) pack of cards had a two shillings and sixpence (12.5p) tax slapped on it.

An official stamp to show duty had been paid, from 1828, was actually the Ace of Spades – known as "Old Frizzle". It is thanks to crippling taxes that decks of this time became scarce and surviving examples are so valuable. If any cards are missing, the value plummets to a tenth of that of a full deck.

JOKER IN THE PACK

The joker was only introduced in the 1860s and comes from a popular American game of the time called "euchre". However, joker collecting is a hobby in itself – so investors should be wary of later packs where the jester is missing.

There are many genres from which to choose. Among the most collectable are those relating to the anti-Catholic Popish Plot that gripped England from 1678 to 1681, sets selling for £700 two decades ago but now for £4000.

Political cards with appeal include a 1983 pack of the main four political parties in Britain – when the SDP was still alive – illustrated by Gerald Scarfe, and which originally cost £4.50 but now sell for £60.

The Worshipful Company of Makers of Playing Cards was granted a charter by King Charles I in 1628 to run a cartel to keep foreign manufacturers out of the British card market. From the late 18th century it began producing a limited set each year. An 1886 deck may fetch £2000 while a 2009 set might be £60.

18th century decks with geographical pictures can fetch £20,000 while 19th century "transformation" decks, where pips (e.g. the diamonds in the 7 of diamonds) form part of an intricate decoration or illustration on the card, could go for £5000.

The 19th century saw a change in card production qualities when the De La Rue printer began rolling out more varieties and designs. Non-picture cards with numbers placed on the card corners, and two-headed picture cards, as well as rounded corners, also started being introduced. These changes made it easier for people to fan and a typical Victorian pack might fetch £100.

Most modern cards are usually worthless but there are exceptions. Coca Cola, Oxo, and Fry's chocolate issued advertising cards in the early 20th century that can sell for £80 a set. Children's games Snap, Happy Families and Whot made in the late 1800s can fetch £50 to £100. A 1930s pack of Walt Disney "Silly Symphony" snap by Chad Valley in good condition may cost £60.

GET A GOOD DEAL

For further information contact the World of Playing Cards (www.wopc.co.uk), or the sister club English Playing Card Society (www.wopc.co.uk/epcs). Reputable traders include InterCol London (www.intercol.co.uk).

Postage Stamps

Philately – stamp collecting and study – is now a world away from its old geeky schoolboy image.

Collectors are enthusiasts from all walks of life with a fascination for history and often a keen business eye. In the past decade top stamps have licked traditional investments with returns averaging more than 10% a year.

Stamp collecting officially began with the issue of the first adhesive stamp Penny Black on May 6 1840, and although they are fantastic pieces of history few are worth more than a few pounds. Stamps used to be cut individually and the imprecise hand of Victorian postal workers means how it was chopped can dramatically affect value – and a used stamp plummets in value. A single Penny Black in mint condition from the corner of a sheet and carrying the plate number could fetch £30,000, while a used one can be picked up for £20. A rare block of ten first-day issue Penny Blacks fetched £200,000 in 1998.

WORLD'S FIRST STAMP

In 1839 a competition to create the world's first stamp attracted 2600 entries, none of which were deemed suitable. The task was then passed to three members of the Royal Academy who came up with a side portrait of 15-year-old Princess Victoria (then a 20-year-old Queen) for the Penny Black.

The two most important attributes are uniqueness and historical importance.

The world record price for a stamp is the £1.3m paid for an 1857 Swedish Treskilling Banco stamp in 1996. The unique selling point is that the stamp was incorrectly printed in yellow instead of the usual green, and the error was so small that there may actually only be one in existence. It has changed hands amongst adventurous investors many times since the 19th century, and was once owned by King Carol of Romania.

Such quirky mistake survivors escalate a stamp's value as the maker usually tries to destroy them as duds. Find one of the a handful of 13p Christmas stamps from 1988 that survived pulping and you could be looking at an investment worth more than £6500. The stamp should have been priced 14p.

The vast majority of modern stamps churned out by Royal Mail are worthless unless they include printing faults. Even first day editions tend to be little more than novelty values as ten are produced every year.

What investors should remember is that just like stocks and shares values can go down as well as up. There was a time in the late Eighties when stamps soared in value and then came down with a crash. Only the most rare and highly sought after stamps are likely to keep their prices if this happens again.

Stamp investors should typically be in it for the long run. In specialist areas where the demand comes from just a few top collectors it can take up to five years to find a buyer through an authorised dealer. Just like buying a second-hand car, the buyer should know about the seller and history of the stamp.

 PHILATELIC LINKS

Check out stamp collector website UK Philately (www.ukphilately.org.uk); Look for traders who are members of the Philatelic Traders' Society (philatelic-traders-society.co.uk); See also the Royal Philatelic Society London (www.rpsl.org.uk) and the Great Britain Philatelic Society (www.gbps.org.uk) Books include *British Stamp Market Values* by Guy Thomas, and *Collect British Stamps* by Stanley Gibbons. Check out *Gibbons Stamp Monthly* magazine.

Postcards

The intrepid Victorian explorer had to travel to Austria if he wanted to send a postcard boasting of his adventures. It was invented there in 1869, but the British Empire was slow to catch on – and the Post Office did not grant the postcard a license until 1894.

The first examples did not offer views of seaside resorts or colourful local scenes but were usually plain with an inky Post Office stamp. It wasn't until 1902, with the introduction of a divided back for both message and address, that pictures on the front became widespread.

The Edwardian era marked a golden age of postcards and this lasted through World War I until 1918, when the ha'penny postage rose to a penny and many people stopped sending the cards.

Top examples of the era with hand-tinted lithographs, chromo litho prints and woven silk cards sell for £20 to £50. A decade ago they may have cost just a fiver. Stumble across an unusual postcard of historical significance and you may have an investment worth far more.

 ## POSTCARD TO EMAIL

During the Edwardian heyday of the postcard, people would use them to send messages much like we might use the phone, a text message or email. The postman would pop round up to seven times a day with mail and a card sent in the morning might arrive in the afternoon.

Nostalgia is the driving force behind the market, with topographical themes showing life in the early 20th century among the most sought after. You might pay £5 for an early seafront view of Brighton but a backstreet shot could be £20 due to rarity and local history interest.

Another collectable area is World War I. Sweethearts shared sequences of sentimental embroidered cards between each other – sequences that sometimes stop abruptly, marking each time a tragic end. WWI prices start at about £5, but those with military crests and battalion insignia can fetch £100 for their unique appeal.

Sport is another key area, including golf, cricket and football. An Edwardian postcard of Manchester United FC that cost £20 a decade ago can now demand £120. Shipping companies in industrial Manchester and Liverpool also offered a huge range of cards, and investors can pay anything from just a few pounds to more than £100 depending on the liner.

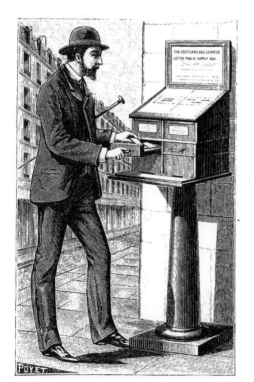

Other popular genres include art deco and Art Nouveau, advertising, animals, railway, cinema, military and comic.

Artist postcards regularly sell for more than £100, with favourites among collectors including Arthur Thiele, Louis Wain, Alphonse Mucha and Toulouse-Lautrec.

Postcards without blemishes are the best investments, but a slightly battered postcard can still be worth money if it bears a poignant message or was sent by someone famous. A postcard by former Beatle John Lennon can sell for £5000 while a card sent by author Franz Kafka went under the hammer a few years ago for £7200.

The most valuable postcards of all are those with historical significance. The highest price ever paid for a postcard is £14,000 in 2002, for one written from the Titanic.

WISH YOU WERE HERE?

Postcards cover every subject so it is a good idea to find a niche area in which to invest. A great place to start and get a feel for the market is visiting one of the regular postcard trading fairs held across the country.

Postcard Traders Association offers details of fairs at www.postcard.co.uk. See the magazine *Picture Postcard Monthly* for trade details and other information (www.postcardcollecting.co.uk). Check out as well Memories Picture Library, Framing and Postcards at www.memoriespostcards.co.uk.

Punk Rock

Punk once stood for anarchy but is now one of the more respectable investments. As a movement punk exploded on to the music and fashion scene of London in the late Seventies. Although the riotous period only lasted about three years, the shockwaves are still felt today.

Original records, posters, clothing and other items relating to the era are now highly sought after thanks to growing interest in this unique period of history. Items once thrown away as rubbish are now worth hundreds or even thousands of pounds.

The most iconic and collectable punk band is The Sex Pistols.

The Sex Pistols were formed in 1975 and only produced four singles and one studio album – "Never Mind the Bollocks" – in the three years of their existence when Johnny Rotten was in the band.

The most valuable is the *God Save the Queen* single cut on the A&M label in 1977 before it dropped them. The Pistols later signed to Virgin, which released the single. The unreleased A&M vinyl is valued at £5000 by *The Rare Record Price Guide* but hit £12,000 at auction.

The publicity materials that surrounded the punk movement are also highly collectable. Auction house Christie's held a rock and roll memorabilia auction in 2008 where a controversial 1976

Sex Pistols tour poster showing genitals fetched £3000. An iconic *God Save the Queen* 1977 promotional poster went for £1875.

Items relating to Sex Pistols bassist Sid Vicious, who died from a heroin overdose in 1979, are among the most collectable – and his signature dramatically pushes up values.

Other punk bands that have a collectable appeal include The Clash, The Damned, The Ramones and New York Dolls. A 1981 promotional poster by The Clash sold for $2750 in America last November while a 1979 signed photo by The Ramones sold for $1250.

PUNKS IN LOVE WITH
MARGARET THATCHER

Contrary to popular opinion, punk is not just a noisy din – that came later when ideas ran out. Obscure punk groups have plenty of original shock appeal that still grabs attention today – and their music is often cheap. Among the quirky punk love ballads are a 1980 single by the Notsensibles called "I'm in love with Margaret Thatcher", which can be purchased for a fiver.

 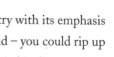

The punk movement revolutionised the clothing fashion industry with its emphasis on experimenting with your own ideas. It didn't matter what you did – you could rip up old garments and stick bits together with safety pins or even dress up in bin-liners – there were, for better or worse, no longer any constraints.

The most sought after punk clothes are those by Vivienne Westwood, who ran a clothes shop in London's King's Road with Sex Pistols manager Malcolm McLaren in the 1970s. Original "Destroy", "Chaos" and "God Save The Queen" t-shirts change hands for more than £500 while the handful of surviving "Rock" and "Perv" t-shirts that used chicken bones to spell out the words under the Let It Rock label might fetch several thousand.

A Sid Vicious signed T-shirt sold for £1300 at auction fives year ago would probably go for double this amount today, as might a pair of Seventies tartan bondage trousers that went for £1528 in 2000.

The fabrics tend to be of poor quality for many garments and often shoddily made. Collectors should only use reputable dealers and be certain of provenance, as the market is flooded with fakes.

 ## NEAT NEAT NEAT INVESTMENTS

This is punk – don't expect it to be easy. Your local record shop may be a good place to insinuate yourself. *Punk: The Definitive Record of a Revolution* by Stephen Colegrave and Chris Sullivan provides a guide to the era, while *The Art of Rock: Posters from Presley to Punk* by Paul Grushkin offers some art examples. Punk rarely comes on the market and much of the trading is done by word-of-mouth through private record shops. Major auction houses such as Christie's do occasionally hold sales, too.

Race Horses

The sport of kings – and Arabs – is also within reach of the hoi polloi. Adventurous investors without the 75,000 guineas or so that may be required for a top thoroughbred can invest in a syndicate for a few hundred a month.

The downside is the same as with most gambling: you are more likely to leave out of pocket than make a fortune. However, investors get the perks of free entry to tracks, training and winning enclosures.

And in the rare punts where you do hit gold the returns can be stratospheric.

 ## WINNER: SIR ALEX FERGUSON

Manchester United manager Sir Alex Ferguson knows how to pick winners off the pitch as well as on it. He went in for a £120,000 half-share of the horse "Rock of Gibraltar" in 2000. Just a couple of years later, having won the Prix de Moulin race in Paris in his seventh consecutive group one win, his investment was estimated to be worth as much as £30m.

LOSER: SHEIKH MOHAMMED

In 1983 Sheikh Mohammed bin Rashid Al Maktoum of Dubai's ruling family splashed out more than $10m (£6.7m) on a yearling colt called Snaafi Dancer. It never won a single race.

The most expensive horses are flat racers and these are usually bought as yearlings – a year old. Investors have been known to pay more than £10m but bargains can be had for less than £40,000. Split this a dozen ways in a syndicate and this might work out at £3000 each.

National Hunt jumpers are cheaper, with horses typically changing hands for less than £20,000 – although those with deep enough pockets can still shell out more than £150,000 for a potential winner.

Don't expect to pay less than £5000 for a strong bet with four legs. After purchase there is then the annual cost of keeping the horse. Stables, vet bills, food, training, blacksmith fees and transport mean a typical additional layout of £15,000 a year must be split among the owners. There may also be initial registration fees to hand over.

The key reward is fun – winnings should be seen as a bonus. Owners typically only recover a fifth of costs but in return get free race entries, and can visit training facilities, stables and winning enclosures.

The part-owner also has a say in horse naming and racing colours.

Investment returns are measured in prize money – with trainer and jockey each taking an average 10% cut – plus any extra value if the horse ends up a winner and is eventually sold off for stud.

JOINING THE SPORT OF KINGS

A syndicate is partnership with up to 20 individuals who share ownership of a horse. However, it can also be racing club membership where you can share the ownership of several horses with risk and reward shared out among thousands. Choose a deal to suit your budget, as it is a gamble and not a sure-fire winner.

Horseracing is not for the faint-hearted and investors should only go into syndicates after doing their homework. Visit trainers and look at a horse before parting with cash. Ensure that the trainer is comfortable with visits and within easy travelling distance if you want to enjoy the full experience of ownership.

The British Horseracing Authority has a directory of partnerships and syndicates across the country available through its website at www.britishhorseracing.com.

Rocking Horses

Bet on an old nag with wooden legs and you might enjoy some great returns – the value of classic rocking horses has as much as quadrupled over the past decade.

Expect to fork out between £1000 and £1500 for a thoroughbred antique rocking horse investment and as much as £3000 for an example in prime condition.

Even injured horses for a few hundred pounds can make money. However, with cheaper horses it may be necessary to additionally invest in an expert restoration that can cost as much as £1000 rather than trust to a budget do-it-yourself – which can often do more harm than good.

The heyday of rocking horses was between 1880 and 1910. The most collectable rocking horse name is FH Ayres. And a swivel-headed Ayres made in 1887 is one of the most sought after of all – they can fetch as much as £20,000 if in great condition.

However, there are plenty of other quality horse makers with good examples costing £1500. In addition to Ayres, these include G&J Lines Brothers and J Collinson & Sons of Liverpool.

Half-moon shaped rockers with horses had been around in England from the 17th century and in the 18th century offered elegantly carved bow-shaped rockers on which children could sit.

The more practical swinging horse fixed on pillars was only invented in America in 1878 but it is on these models that most collectors tend to focus as the static-stand means they are more practical for the modern home.

When checking the quality of a horse, look for glass eyes and real horsehair as a sign of a good maker. The elegance of the carving and quality of the top plate holding the swinging irons on to the wooden top bars are also telltale signs of quality.

The dapple grey rocking horse favoured by Victorian children continues to hold the greatest appeal. Many of these earliest beasts, which strained at the reins with ferocious teeth-baring snarls, might not appeal to youngsters of a nervous disposition.

An important quality of a good horse is that you are able to sit on its back and enjoy a regular ride – and if you purchase a big horse, even large adults can enjoy it. Purchasing a horse just to look at is a great shame, as it needs plenty of exercise.

Typical abuse to old horses included the trimming of manes and tails by over eager youngsters and leather harnesses and saddles becoming worn with age. Chipped paintwork is often also a victim once more to poor restoration; damage can be made more grievous by a fresh lick of paint.

THE FIRST ROCKING HORSE

The rocking horse goes back thousands of years; even the Egyptian boy-king Tutankhamun is believed to have had one when he was growing up. Roman youngsters often had their own toy steed to ride, before getting the real thing.

Modern handmade rocking horses also hold their value and should grow in appeal over time. In addition, they have the attraction of already being in good condition and complying with modern safety standards.

However, although they tend to be cheaper than Victorian examples they are rarely as well made as the best earlier models. A hundred years ago craftsmen served long apprenticeships and relied on the skills of their hands rather than modern equipment.

Would-be investors might also like to try their hand at making a rocking horse themselves if they cannot afford to purchase a wooden nag ready-made. It can be a rewarding pastime and great opportunity to create a family heirloom. However, skill and patience are not the only qualities that are required, as necessary carving tools will cost more than £100.

BETTING ON A WOODEN NAG

Just like when you bet on any real-life horse, study the form first. Books that can help include *The Complete Rocking Horse Maker* by Anthony Dew and *The Rocking Horse: A History of Moving Toy Horses* by Patricia Mullins and Narisa Chakra. Traders include the Rocking Horse Workshop (www.rockinghorses.co.uk) and the Rocking Horse Shop (www.rockinghorse.co.uk).

Royal Memorabilia

Gawd bless you Ma'am, and all who invest in your commemorative mugs and other patriotic paraphernalia. While most royalty spin-offs are little more than mass-produced junk, there are a few gems that can justify pride of place on the mantelpiece. In the past decade collectable values have typically risen by no more than 10%, but the most rare items can buck this trend.

Typically, it is necessary to wait at least half a century for most pieces of pottery to be worth a substantial sum.

Artist Eric Ravilious is the most sought after name behind 20th century royal mugs. A Wedgwood cup commemorating the never-to-happen coronation of Edward VIII can now fetch more than £1000. The heir to the thrown was prohibited from becoming king after he told the government he intended to marry the American divorcee Wallis Simpson in 1936. Ravilious' style was so popular that even though he was killed in World War II his skills and designs were still copied for the 1953 coronation of Queen Elizabeth II.

Another earlier crisis that attracts investor interest due to scarcity and historic significance is the coronation mug for Edward VII dated accurately for August

1902. This fetches more than twice the price of the much more widely-produced memorabilia for the original coronation date of June 26th (which was delayed amidst fears the prince would die after he went down with appendicitis).

Royal memorabilia can be traced to the coronation of King Charles II in 1661, when ceremonial pomp was encouraged after a ten-year stretch of puritanical leadership under Parliamentarian Oliver Cromwell. Examples of these hand-made and hand-painted royal memorabilia plates – tin-glazed earthenware English delft – are extremely rare and fetch more than £60,000. Mugs were not yet in fashion, but collectors could instead pick up a royally jubilant bleeding bowl: a half-moon shaped shaving dish used by barbers.

The coronation of Queen Victoria in 1837 marked the start of the golden age of collecting royal memorabilia and this mug is now worth £1400. Few people knew what their monarch actually looked like so a portrait on a cup or plate was something in which to take real pride.

The Queen reigned over the British Empire's most successful era and memorabilia from her 64 years on the throne is still the most in demand. However, because so many items were churned out during her lengthy reign, she is also not always the most valuable.

Like all commemorative pottery, a chip or crack can make an item almost worthless, so it is important to buy examples that look as good as new. Mugs come in all shapes and sizes, with two-handled loving cups and three-handled tygs often being the most valuable because they are the easiest to break.

A MUG'S GAME

A Spitting Image Prince Charles mug available for £2 in 1981 might now fetch £200 in top condition. The mug is rare as its pottery ears often got knocked off.

Many potteries earned their royal seals of approval for being so patriotic, such as Doulton for praising Queen Victoria on its 1897 Diamond Jubilee mugs. Potters to look out for include Wedgwood, Royal Worcester, Royal Doulton, Colport, Minton, Copeland Spode, Royal Crown Derby, Moorcroft, Davenport and Royal Delft. Investors should avoid Franklin Mint.

GOD SAVE YOUR INVESTMENT

A reputable specialist dealer can offer free valuations as well as keeping an eye out for a chosen item. Haggle for a realistic price. Contact: royalty trader Sue Rees on (01582) 715 555; or the Commemorative Collectors Society at www.commemorativescollecting.co.uk.

Rupert Bear

Why not join Rupert Bear and his friends Bill Badger, Algy Pug, the impish Raggety, and Pong-Ping for a magical adventure in Nutwood in search of a real pot of gold?

Despite never changing out of his yellow checked trousers, matching scarf, and red jumper, Rupert has confounded fashion critics over the ages with his best-selling annuals. Vintage copies regularly change hands for thousands of pounds and, thanks to the recent launch of a new Rupert TV show, a fresh generation of fans may soon be joining the fray.

Rupert began life as a *Daily Express* strip drawn by Mary Tourtel in November 1920. Artist Alfred Bestall took over in 1935 and made the character his own for the next 30 years – creating 270 adventures before retiring at the age of 90. The earliest newspaper strips were not initially bound in annuals, but in Monster Rupert books. A well looked-after example can still be picked up – for about £1000. *The New Adventures of Rupert* is the first true annual and appeared in 1936. A well looked-after copy in original dust wrapper can fetch £2500 but without might be £400.

Rupert fought on through the war to boost morale but paper scarcity, and limited print runs, has helped bump up the price of these annuals. Particularly sought after is the 1939 copy where traditional red cloth binding was dropped in favour of pink to save on ink dye. Expect to pay up to £1200 for a top example.

But the most valuable Rupert annual of all is the proof run of a dozen 1973 annuals with a brown faced Rupert on the cover, which has fetched £23,000 at auction. The *Express* ordered Rupert to be painted white for the full print run. Rupert has always kept a brown face on the cover of all the other annuals published – though he always appears white on the inside for the cartoon strips.

Key to his attraction is longing for a now bygone age – with a modest but perhaps important moral message in the fabulous stories, and their celebration of the spirit of friendship and adventure without the need for violence, horror or crassness to hold the reader's interest. It is wholesome escapism at its best. Be warned, though: in his TV reincarnation Rupert has appalled the purists by wearing a pair of trainers. Disgraceful.

A RUPERT IN EVERY FRAME

When Alfred Bestall turned up to illustrate the strip he was told he must write the stories as well. Fortunately, the artist turned out to be a real natural. Central to his compelling style is his insistence on showing Rupert in every frame – even if it is just an ear or a hand.

Condition is key: a well-thumbed edition may be worth a tenth of the value of a top-notch example. Only invest if thrilled by Rupert Bear and his bizarre chums. Rupert's adventures have been immortalised within the pages of 50m books sold worldwide, so it won't be too hard to experimentally pick up an annual for just a few pounds to get a flavour. Modern facsimile editions of the annuals are also available brand new from most bookshops.

The *Express* sold its controlling stake in Rupert in 2005 to Entertainment Rights, which created the TV series "Rupert Bear, Follow the Magic...". The new owners may push the character on to the US market. Just like Winnie the Pooh, Rupert may one day pick up an American accent – but if it is a success the value of his collectables are likely to soar.

FOLLOW THE MAGIC

Buy off a reputable second-hand bookshop or trader and be wary of over-hyped annuals on internet auction sites. Invest pre-Eighties and the best you can afford. Get help from the Rupert Bear Fan Club at www.rupertthebear.org.uk.

Russian Dolls

Paradoxically, ever-decreasing returns can be a great investment with Russian dolls – the dolls that get smaller and smaller are going up and up in value.

Matryoshka nesting dolls are hollow wooden figures that once pulled apart reveal another smaller character stacked inside. The traditional hand-decorated treasures hold at least five separate figures though they can boast up to 30. In the last five years an explosion in interest has seen top examples of these dolls soar three-fold in value and they now regularly fetch £1000 or more.

A top quality example can take three months of pain-staking work: it requires a unique skill to hand-paint the characters in three-dimension on to a curved pieced of wood. So Russian Matryoshka dolls in their native land are not actually toys but valuable ornaments often given away as wedding and christening gifts.

These fine collectable pieces are not to be confused with the crudely painted red-and-yellow "Seminov" sets sold in tourist shops or novelty examples that depict politicians or celebrities.

The history of the Matryoshka dates back to about 1890 from an idea starting in Japan. The Russian dolls combine Japanese deity character ideas with those of the Fabergé egg of the period – layers including yolk, egg, hen and crown. Painter Sergei Maliutin painted the first of these and they are now priceless museum pieces.

Before communism, Russian saints were the main theme. But after the first Russian revolution in 1912 the painting of icons was suppressed. This is why most collectable dolls throughout the Soviet period depict Russian folk tales.

Classics such as Alionuskha (a story of a boy turned into a goat), Peter and the Wolf, Masha and the Bear (the foundation of Little Red Riding Hood), and The Firebird are among the most sought after. These stories are wonderful but it is the skill of the artist in depicting them that is the most important consideration.

MATRYOSHKA

The name Matryoshka means mother and she is typically the portly peasant figure who holds the family within – being a figure of motherhood and fertility. Stripping away the layers also often reveals a tale told through depictions on the peasant figures' aprons.

It is the skill of the artwork that counts and not the number of dolls inside. Quality collectable examples typically start at £40 but the most sought after examples go for over £1000.

Look for finely crafted dolls made in the USSR rather than Russia as these can be particularly valuable. Examples of the best finely decorated pieces can command four-figures as they were rare in the Soviet era, a period when artists were crushed and mass produced state-approved dolls were churned out by factories.

Even nowadays prices of examples by top artists, such as Valentina Stepkayova, are rising sharply thanks to changes in the Russian economy turning a time-consuming highly skilled tradition into a potentially dying art form.

SEEKING DECREASING RETURNS

St Petersburg is a fabulous place for the adventurous investor to start their collection and a great excuse for a short break. Books include *Matryoshka – Russian Souvenirs* by M. Chereiskaya; *The Art of the Russian Matryoshka* by Rett Ertl, Rick Hibberd and Yakov Chitov. Traders include www.babooshkashop.co.uk.

Seaside Sauce

No sex please, we're British – this was once our watchword. But the world of nudge-nudge humour – where the jokes are risqué and double-entendres abound – if perhaps somewhat smutty, can now be worth good money.

Politically incorrect, and a little racy for those of a traditional disposition, the unique British gags of bathing beauties, battle-axes, weedy husbands and nudist colonies can be turned into a great adventurous investment.

The sauce seems most at home on the seaside pier. It arose there in the wake of the straight-laced world of the Victorian prude, when the seaside health resort began providing holiday escapism at the turn of the 20th century.

Innovations such as the what-the-butler-saw machines, where viewers could enjoy private titillation for just a penny, now turn over for thousands of pounds. Meanwhile, innuendo-laden seaside cards that were once banned by local councils for being obscene can change hands for £20 or more.

And stumble across original saucy art from a top illustrator such as Donald McGill and you may have a piece of art valued at £3000.

King of the comic seaside card – "Picasso of the Pier" – Donald McGill began publishing saucy classics in 1912 with a 'They've got 'em in all shapes and sizes' cartoon of bathing beauties. He followed up in 1914 with a chambermaid peeping through a bathroom keyhole assuring a waiting guest, 'He won't be long now, sir, he's drying himself.'

Over five decades he produced more than 12,000 different cartoons and sold over 200m cards. Because there were so many they can still be picked up for just a few quid; even the earliest ones are available at about £20, despite being sought after.

In 1954 he was brought to court on an obscenity charge for peddling smut. McGill pleaded guilty and was fined £50 at the Lincoln assizes. He died in 1962.

Although McGill is seen as the godfather of sauce there are plenty of other highly valued postcard illustrators, including Douglas Tempest, Arnold Taylor and Brian Fitzpatrick.

Picking the right theme is key. You and others need to be able to get the joke, and the particularly good ones fetch more. Jewish jokes and black humour, of late, have tended to do particularly well. Also, gags relating to professions like dental or legal work are perennial favourites.

McGill watercolours can fetch £1000, while the record for cheek is the £3850 paid in 1994 for an original 'Hey Sonia' postcard by Yorkshire firm James Bamford. It pictured an ice skater being hailed by a friend for forgetting her underwear.

SAUCY SECRET

A collection of 40,000 seaside snaps and postcards packed with naughty puns and gags owned by comic Ronnie Barker were sold anonymously at auction for £60,000 in 2007.

The mutoscope was patented in 1894 and soon nicknamed the "what-the-butler-saw" machine, for its coin-in-the-slot peepshows. The antique stand-alone machines can fetch £2000 at auction, and next to today's deviance they provide a quaint glimpse of a rather more innocent age. It is this relatively innocent erotica and historical novelty value that makes them so collectable.

Made of cast iron, they had a drum of static photos that, when turned in quick succession by cranking a handle, would show a 45-second glimpse of something titillating. The thrills viewers enjoyed under titles such as 'Lady at her Boudoir' included women getting out of a bath, or pulling off a pair of stockings.

GET IN THE MOOD

The out-of-print book *Sauce* by Ronnie Barker is an excellent place to start. Mutoscopes and original prints occasionally turn up at auction. For saucy cards check out *Picture Postcard Monthly* at www.postcardcollecting.co.uk.

Scalextric

Ahobby can become a full-throttle investment with vintage slot car racers. It is not just a sport for kids but enjoys a huge adult following among plastic track speed kings – as well as a growing number amongst adventurous investors.

Prices of top slot cars have typically doubled over the past decade thanks to a wave of nostalgia and modern set improvements both fuelling a huge revival of interest.

The most sought after racing cars are Scalextric from the Sixties, when vehicles often ended smashed on skirting boards by Boxing Day. Surviving motors can fetch thousands of pounds while even old bits of track from that era are worth some money.

Scalextric was an instant success when it was first launched in 1957, employing tin-plated vehicles and strong rubber tracks – as a spin-off from Scalex wind-up cars. An original boxed set will typically fetch £500.

But from 1960 the slot cars were made of plastic. These later cars were far more vulnerable but with more interesting designs. By teatime on Christmas most had been involved in accidents and sparked off the traditional family row.

It means that those few vehicles that have survived the festivities of the Sixties unscathed and were the most iconic designs are now in high demand from slot car investors.

The holy grail of Scalextric motors is the Bugatti model made in 1964, which was pulled off the shelves because it so easily broke. It is now worth up to £3000. However, if you stumble across an unopened James Bond set from the mid-Sixties, complete with Aston Martin racers, it might fetch as much as £3500 at auction.

Even a piece of old track from the Sixties – such as an obsolete piece of the Goodwood Motor Circuit track chicane – can be worth as much as £200.

Rarity alone is not the primary consideration. Certain models are more appealing than others, just like with full-scale cars, and this pushes up prices. Although not particularly rare, a 1964 Austin Healey can fetch £150 because of its looks. Other popular models include Aston Martin DB4 and Mercedes 190.

Colour is also important. A 1964-manufactured 1933 Alfa Romeo painted blue might fetch £150 while a yellow example can be worth £500.

SPEED KING

Scalextric competition racers soup up engines to reach speeds of 80 mph. These supercharged cars cost hundreds of pounds but do not typically climb in value like vintage motors – though they can provide equal thrills for the cash.

Condition is key to value – only by picking the best surviving examples can you treat them as investments. Used cars are far better for having fun on the tracks. Watch out, though, as the quality of cars in the late Seventies and Eighties was often poor and so they tend to hold much less allure.

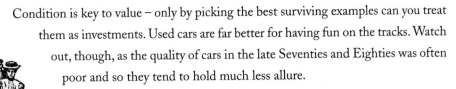

Foreign competitors such as Fly and Ninco started producing better quality slot cars than Scalextric in the Eighties and these are collectable in their own right.

Fortunately, Scalextric has enjoyed a renaissance in recent years, which has helped boost the vintage market, partly thanks to the manufacturing of new digital sets that allow cars to switch lanes, thus heightening the strategy and realism of the game.

 ## GET TRIGGER HAPPY

Indispensable industry guide *Scalextric: The Definitive Guide*, written by Roger Gillham, provides a full history and details of collectables and is a great starting point. Although bargains can be found on the internet, novice investors should first deal through an established trader. Contact National Scalextric Collectors Club, www.nscc.co.uk. Also check out the British Slot Car Racing Association, www.bscra.fsnet.co.uk.

Scientific Instruments

The Victorian gentleman adventurer enjoyed collecting a wide range of scientific accessories. Strategically placed around the study, they were largely designed to impress high-minded guests, and only occasionally used for research.

Modern enthusiasts are rediscovering their early scientific appeal. Microscopes, telescopes, globes, medical devices and all manner of scientific paraphernalia have soared in value since the modern market took off in the early Nineties.

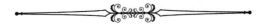

Dutch scientist Antonie van Leeuwenhoek is regarded as the father of the microscope. His late 17th century microscopes are nondescript items the size of a 50p piece but can sell for more than £100,000.

The Victorian era was the golden age for microscopes. Makers such as Ross, R&J Beck and Powell & Lealand are among the best for quality investments. While if you want something to really look the part, how about a giant brass four-footer by Moritz Pillischer from the 1850s? It will set you back £5000.

Those on a budget can also find great 19th century microscopes from names such as Watson and Leitz from about £500, while unbranded microscopes cost a fraction of the price.

Victorian hobby scientists took their microscope obsessions to amusing lengths. They would study full-stop sized photographs – ranging from Queen Victoria to naughty erotica. These fascinating miniscule slides can be picked up as novelty investments for just a few pounds.

Hans Lipperhey patented the telescope in 1608. Two years later Galileo was making his observations that got him charged with heresy by the Roman Catholic church for discovering the earth is not at the centre of the universe.

However, it is the classic 18th century portable multi-draw brass telescopes, often decorated in black or green leather, sometimes in sharkskin, that investors most want to put to their eye.

The 18th and 19th century makers such as Dollond, George Adam, Nairne, Simms and Troughton can command anything from a few hundred to thousands of pounds.

Globes made decorative objects and not just scientific instruments. They have as much as quadrupled in value over the past two decades. Terrestrials sell better than celestial, fetching double the price. Prices start at a few hundred pounds but 18th and 19th century globes from top makers like George Adams as well as John & William Cary can cost many thousands.

Pocket globes are also highly sought after and a three-inch 18th century Nathaniel Hill – with America as "unknown parts" – can change hands for £5000.

The record price paid is £1m in 1991 for a pair of 16th century gilt metal globes made by the cartographer Gerardus Mercator for the Turkish Sultan Murad III.

 ## DRILLING FOR DEVILS

Trepanning was a common medical practice in the 18th and 19th century, involving a hole the size of a 10p piece being drilled into the skull. The aim was to release the devils of despair – melancholy – and alleviate epileptic fits. Rather paradoxically, you might think, it was also used to cure headaches. Antique trepanning kits start at £1000, though early drilling sets have been known to sell for up to £13,000.

There is a huge variety of collectable medical instruments out there – including ear trumpets, surgery saws, tooth extraction keys and bleeding bowls. They can all be picked up for £200 upwards.

However, decorated leech jars that might have been purchased for £200 a couple of decades ago now often sell for £2000 or more due to their unique appeal.

Investment quality scientific instruments must be in full working order and ideally with the original wooden cabinet in which they were typically stored. If you look hard you can see the original brush marks. Beware of re-polished and re-lacquered items; such renovations can knock off more than half the price. Chipped or cracked lenses for microscopes and telescopes should be avoided but an expert can easily clean dirty glasses to transform their value.

AN EYE FOR SCIENCE

The international Antique Science and Early Technology & Medical Instrument Fair regularly held in London is a great place to begin (www.scientificfair.com). Specialist dealers include Elizabeth & Desmond Squire at www.scienceantiques.com. Clubs include The Scientific Instrument Society (www.sis.org.uk).

Scotch Whisky

Canny investors may enjoy tasty returns from a wee dram of whisky. Over the past decade the niche market of single malt Scotch whisky has enjoyed overall returns of up to 20% on the average vintage bottle.

At the top end of the market, where whisky is at least 50 years old or more, the record price so far paid is £32,000 in 2002 for a bottle of Dalmore Single Malt. This was the amount handed over by a visiting connoisseur to the Pennyhill Park Hotel in Surrey, who then sat back and drank it with a group of friends.

Macallan released a 50-year old whisky in the early Eighties for about £60 a bottle – which might now go for £7000 a piece.

Even later vintages, such as a limited edition Black Bowmore distilled in 1964 and released in 1993 at £80 a bottle, can now change hands for as much as £2000.

You can invest in whisky in a bottle or cask. Bottled whisky is the more popular choice.

Those investing in bottles should look to limited editions. Serious labels to look out for include Bowmore, Bruichladdich, Glenfiddich, Springbank, Talisker, The Balvenie and The Macallan. Others, highly collectable because the distilleries have now closed, include Brora, Dallas Dhu and Glen Flagler.

A cask has the potential tax advantage of avoiding duty if sold back to the producers and kept in a bonded warehouse. You are investing in 250 litres at a cost of typically at least £1000. When it reaches the shops several years later it may be worth £2500. However, seek expert advice first as the market has been hit with whisky scams in the past. Also be aware that there may be a storage rental fee, typically £20 a year.

THE ANGEL'S SHARE

Whisky must be kept in a cask in bond for at least three years before it can be called whisky, but is usually kept in barrels for a decade or more. If a whisky is described as 60-years-old this is the time it would have spent in a cask before being bottled. The cask is what gives the whisky spirit all its taste and colour. About 2% evaporates while in storage – known as "the angel's share".

Although a rare and historic bottle may be worth thousands of pounds this is no guarantee it will be drinkable. A sign to look out for is the level of whisky in the bottle. If it is high this is a good sign; but down to the shoulder or label and it may have oxidised and be flat.

Whisky does not go off over time like wine but should still be kept at a standard room temperature away from direct sunlight and heat. It is also advisable to occasionally wet the cork to prevent it from shrinking.

Whiskey was first drunk in Ireland by monks in the 5th century before such holy skills were transferred over to Scotland. Malt Scotch has a distinctive style, derived from malted barley and yeast in a pot still distillation.

AVOID WHISKY ON THE ROCKS

There is no investment market for blended whisky and a single malt Scotch is what you need – though a standard 10-year-old will never rise in value.

There is no point in investing in whisky unless you like it because part of the appeal is the fun of enjoying the samples. It is fine to add water to a top single malt but not ice: this freezes the aroma.

A good place to begin is specialist publication *Whisky Magazine*, www.whiskymag.com. There are plenty of auction houses and specialist retailers, including The Whisky Exchange, www.thewhiskyexchange.com.

Share Certificates

Scripophily? It may sound like a rather ancient pursuit – Greek for "love of stock" – but the term to describe the art of collecting old bonds and share certificates was only coined in 1978.

The market attracts barely 20,000 enthusiasts worldwide but has enjoyed remarkable returns in recent years for long-dead share certificates. Although a company may no longer exist, esoteric old certificates can be worth a great deal as unique pieces of capitalist history. Some papers are also beautiful pieces of art with handwritten signatures from great historic figures.

A first issue of the Standard Oil Company from 1871 with the signature of its famous president John D. Rockefeller can sell for more than £100,000. It could have been picked up for £3000 in the late Eighties.

Although American certificates tend to be the most colourful and flamboyant, British examples also have their own unique charm.

Some 17th century British certificates – such as those for Welsh iron companies – were printed on vellum (goatskin). While others, such as those of the Lancashire cotton mills, offer insights into an area once packed with 400 thriving mills. Even the most sought after cotton mill certificates tend to fetch no more than £150 – but that value has still risen ten-fold over the past 20 years.

Empire expansion is a popular theme among investors, as are railways, grand engineering projects and mining. But the holy grail of old share certificates is from the first voyage to India by the East India Company in 1601, none of which are known to exist.

Although the history of share certificates can be plotted back thousands of years to ancient Mesopotamia, the modern equivalent only began around 1600 when bond issues were sold for international trade adventures. Collectors tend to lose interest in share issues after the start of World War II.

When looking to buy old certificates look at a variety of factors, such as decorative quality, historic importance and autographs. You should also only buy paper in top condition to boost investment potential.

Find an area that you might be interested in, such as a geographical location or type of business that might spur you on to doing further research. It is worth doing your homework otherwise you will get lost in something of a maze.

 ## BIRTH OF LONDON STOCK EXCHANGE

In the 17th century, commodity bartering turned to share dealing. In 1698 – just 11 years after the opening of Lloyd's coffee house and the start of the insurance market – Daniel Edwards opened a coffee shop where company shares with certificates were traded in the first London Stock Exchange.

Since the fall or diminution of traditional communism, older Russian and Chinese certificates have seen meteoric price rises. This is because ownership and trading of historic mementos from Imperial China and Tsarist Russia had been outlawed during the cold war era when any reference with the capitalist past was seen as subversive.

Some companies still listed on the London Stock Exchange as worthless stock gave shareholders a totally unexpected windfall of several thousand pounds after the fall of the USSR in the Eighties. This was because to re-enter the international business arena they were forced to honour long-forgotten debts for companies that had been in mothballs for more than a hundred years.

SHARE AND SHARE ALIKE

Do your homework to ensure you do not get lost in a confusing mountain of choice: a key part of the appeal is the detective work required when delving into the history of names of companies on the bonds.

For further information and details of dealers contact the International Bond and Share Society via website www.scripophily.org. It offers catalogues for what is available and the prices. The book *Scripophily: The Art of Finance* by Keith Hollender, is a great starting point for novice investors.

Shrunken Heads

Intrepid British explorers first infiltrated the Jivaro region deep in the Ecuadorian Peruvian Amazon in the 1850s. Learning that the local culture believed shrunken heads brought good luck they then, naturally, started to buy them. The 19th century exchange rate was a musket for a shrunken head, an acceptable deal for a tribe that had previously fought with only bows, arrows and spears.

These shrunken heads became so popular that (rather grimly) many were made to order to satisfy demand, with the business expanding across Panama, Ecuador, Columbia and Peru. By the mid-20th century the price had risen to £20 for a shrunken head. By the 1990s they were changing hands for between £2000 and £3000 each. White heads were even more valuable.

The exhibition firm Ripley's Believe It Or Not paid $15,000 for a head once reported to have belonged to author Ernest Hemingway. Present-day adventurous investors can expect to pay £5000 for an authentic shrunken head – if they can find one.

The Jivaro Indians, an Amazonian tribe, stand out for their skill at shrinking heads – an art they called "tsantsa".

According to the Spanish Conquistadors these head-shrinkers were 'the only race crueller than nature'. (The Conquistadors were naturally somewhat cold in their views after the Jivaros poured molten gold down the throat of a Spanish governor until he burst. The Jivaros then slaughtered every nearby Spanish woman and child.)

The heads of the enemy were taken by the Jivaro as trophies with a belief that it could improve their warrior powers – thanks to the magical power "tsarutama". The heads would then be treated to trap the soul of the conquered victim.

The practice was outlawed in the 20th century.

Other areas in the world where head shrinking was practised include the region of Nagaland in eastern India and north-west Burma, where the Naga tribe live. New Zealand Maori and tribes from East Timor have also shrunk heads – but most of their headhunting was more concerned with preservation rather than shrinking *per se*.

Genuine shrunken heads are far more rare than forgeries, which account for 80% of the market. A real head is a leathery murder victim the size of a fist. Forgers use old corpses, heads of monkeys and sloths. Leather replicas are not valuable.

 ## HOW TO SHRINK A HEAD

The head is treated close to death – sometimes the treatment is what kills them. Decapitated just below the neck, the head is then cut up the back and the face peeled off. The skin is turned inside out and scraped clean, with the eyes, mouth and back of neck sewn up. Skull and brain are discarded. The skin is simmered in a pot of berry-cured water for an hour and a half until tightened and shrunken to a third of its natural size. Heated pebbles, hot sand and red seeds are put inside and the skin is moisturised. The head is smoked over a fire for the night and the skin treated with charcoal ash. Decorative beads are often added to the shrunken head.

GETTING AHEAD OF THE GAME

The exhibiting of shrunken heads used to be common but is now rare. Most auction houses refuse to *openly* sell them. Shrunken heads can still, though, occasionally be found through tribal art dealers. It is a taboo trade in South America.

Ski Posters

Ski posters have enjoyed thrilling off-piste returns over the past decade, with prices soaring as much as ten-fold in value. Enthusiasts regularly pay thousands for their evocative appeal.

The history of skiing stretches back hundreds of years but it wasn't until the early 20th century that it became widely recognised as a recreational sport. To entice wealthy Europeans to newly created ski slopes holiday posters were produced for travel agents and station platforms showing the glamour and excitement of French and Swiss resorts. The most stylish posters capture far more than just the early days of a fabulous sport but also offer stunning examples of daring art deco.

Images around the Alps are among the most collectable. Early 20th century posters advertising the wealthiest resorts, such as St Moritz in Switzerland and Chamonix in France, tend to attract most attention for capturing a stylish time in sporting history.

In the Thirties these were joined by the new jet-set destinations of Klosters, Davos, Gstaad and Zermatt, in Switzerland.

There were some really talented artists in this era whose well-looked after posters can command five-figure sums. Swiss artist Martin Peikert is highly sought after for his breathtaking mountain scenes and vivid colours, while fellow Swiss Emil Cardinaux and Dutchman Roger Broders are also iconic poster art greats.

Another top 20th century artist is Frenchman Paul Ordner, who turned pummel lifts into art, plus Swiss artist Alex Diggelmann and French artist Bernard Villemot, who painted in a Manet-style.

Although these early posters may be out of financial reach for many pockets, later posters from the Fifties and Sixties are still collectable for a few hundred pounds.

This later time was the dawn of the mass ski holiday. Some of the most interesting posters of the period have fascinating photographs with great retro appeal.

The record price for a ski poster is £36,500 handed over in early 2008 for a 1952 picture of a downhill race in Russia that had an estimate of £600. But this was an exception to the rule that tends to focus on the golden years of ski posters, the 1920s and 1930s, and those featuring luxury European resorts.

It was an era where you bumped into millionaire playboys escorting glamorous models wrapped in furs and diamonds rather than the less exciting middle class après ski crowds and snowboarders that fill the slopes today.

In 2004 an investor handed over £23,900 for a 1920s view of the Palace Hotel in St Moritz by Emil Cardinaux. In 2000 the same poster was sold for £2000.

A 1935 Carl Moos poster of a flying ski jumper in St Moritz fetched £12,000 when it went under the hammer about five years ago.

RIPPING RETURNS

The superb quality of the lithographic prints means the limited numbers of posters can be worth as much as the artist's original work. This is because once the ski season was over posters were ripped down and binned. Very few have survived the ravages of time.

Investors should be particularly wary of buying posters reported to be original as the internet market is awash with fakes that are actually reprints.

However, professionally restored original posters are still valuable. This should include having them linen-backed, at an extra cost of about £100. Unlike some investments, a well looked after poster can be hung up and enjoyed as a work as art as long as is behind ultra-violet glass or plastic.

TAKING IT OFF-PISTE

Deal with professional traders and auction houses to avoid fakes. Reputable dealers include www.originalskiposters.com; Christopher & Co, of Aspen, US, www.christopherco.com; and Omnibus Gallery, Aspen, Colorado, www.omnibusgallery.com. Christie's in London holds a ski poster sale each winter.

Stuffed Animals

There is far more to taxidermy than moth-eaten specimens collecting dust. Since British artist Damien Hirst began pickling sharks and cows in formaldehyde in the early Nineties, stuffing animals has regained a cutting edge image last seen in the Edwardian age. This has sent values of top collectables soaring.

Quality cabinet exhibits that were sometimes thrown out as junk as little as a decade ago have risen as much as tenfold in value and can fetch thousands of pounds. The most skilled Victorian taxidermists are typically the best investments. Peter Spicer of Leamington Spa, James Rowland Ward of London, TE Gunn of Norwich, Edward Gerrard of London, J Hutchings of Aberystwyth are all top names to keep an eagle eye out for.

Examples by these great taxidermists, such as foxes and badgers, costing £400 at the turn of the millennium, can go for £4000, while a highly sought after snowy owl kept in tip-top condition might sell for as much as £5000.

But remember, the vast majority of old taxidermy examples are poor and it is these unnatural and often macabre pieces that have given the industry a bad reputation.

Modern examples from the best taxidermists have also been rising in value, with prices as much as doubling in the past couple of years. It is not the animal or bird that is important but the quality of taxidermy that matters most.

You can have a golden eagle badly stuffed worth little more than a tenner while a couple of sparrows expertly handled might cost up to £2000.

As a collector you should always invest in quality. You can spend as little as £300 for a modern common owl taxidermy example or up to £5000 for an eagle.

Birds are among the most collectable for taxidermy enthusiasts. Along with owls, kingfishers, birds of prey and game birds typically most in demand.

You must look for something that retains a spirit of life and has nothing unnatural about it. View it as a piece of art that breathes life with a natural pose. It should be set within a quality cabinet and good scenery.

There is nothing exploitative or cruel about modern taxidermy, as all animals are accounted for and nothing purposely killed. The Department for Environment, Food and Rural Affairs (DEFRA) regulates taxidermy and since 1947 importing of almost all animals has been illegal.

Victorian exotic animals should usually be avoided – they are probably too politically incorrect now. Hunting trophies, for the same reason, also tend not to rise in value. Less contentious genres where antique values have risen include butterflies, insects, birds, fish and turtles.

However, there is still a market for animals that were collected in the Victorian era and are now often close to extinction. A complete lion might cost £11,000, a tiger's head £2000 and a well looked after crocodile up to £5000.

DON'T STUFF THE PET

Don't stuff your own pet. Please. A loving memory may be turned into a macabre mistake. If you must, a quality cat stuffing typically costs at least £1000 and a dog would be double this price. It won't rise in value.

Interest in taxidermy peaked in the Victorian era, as people were keen to share in the adventure of foreign animals but seldom went abroad. They also had an interest in small animals set up in human poses and clothes – a Victorian whimsy. A sale at Walter Potter's Museum of Curiosities at the Jamaica Inn, Cornwall, in 2003 included a Walter Potter tableau of 37 stuffed kittens sitting around a dinner table and playing croquet. It sold at the auction for £18,800. The Death and Burial of Cock Robin fetched £25,000.

Celebrity stuffed animals also have a market. The grizzly bear that starred with Steptoe and Son in their BBC TV sitcom went under the hammer for £7638, while a ferret that crawled up Compo's leg in the BBC TV comedy *Last of the Summer Wine* went for £411, both at the same 2003 auction.

GETTING STUFFED

UK Guild of Taxidermists, at www.taxidermy.org.uk, provides advice and details of traders and taxidermists, plus courses on how to stuff animals.

Swords

The pen is mightier than the sword? Splendid nonsense. When it comes to weapons of choice, few warriors win by flourishing a ballpoint pen in the face of the enemy. To survive to write the tale, a trusty blade with a glinting edge is always the clear winner. And in investment, though we have seen good returns on fountain pens, cold steel is again a more than worthy competitor.

Investors focus on specific eras and styles, with the majority of English swords dating from the 14th century. Early medieval examples, such as 10th century Viking swords, tend to have starting prices of about £5000.

The sword of the 18th century is highly collectable, prices typically varying between £500 and £5000, depending on condition and quality. Values remain strong because, although still deadly weapons, the swords were by now also status symbols and some possess finely decorated silver hilts inlaid with gems.

Swords from the Napoleonic wars also hold special appeal and values continue to rise due to the fascination accorded to this swashbuckling time of military conflict. Some received swords for valour in battle and these can sell for £50,000 or more.

The sword began defining history 5000 years ago when copper and bronze weapons with leaf-shaped blades started sorting out tribal arguments. When the Romans arrived we went on to straight double-edged blades and ornate hilt handles.

Between about 1100AD and 1800AD the Damascus sword forged in the Middle East held legendary status as the most skilful yet ruthless work of steel-forged art. It could cleave a floating silk scarf as easily as a knight's body.

By the 16th century we had stopped just hacking and were getting more interested in intricate swordplay. Swords that could cut through armour meant the tip and not just the edge were used and this led to slimmer blades and fancy hilts.

Small swords fell out of fashion as the weapon of choice during the 18th century when the gun became the popular choice for a quick kill. However, as a ceremonial accessory it continued to develop as a piece of deadly beauty.

  ## SAMURAI AND SEPPUKU

Japanese Samurai warriors went to work with a katana (sword) and tanto (knife). To avoid falling into enemy hands, and all the consequent shame, the samurai could commit seppuku (suicide). The tanto was used by the Samurai to cut open the abdomen, while an assistant would finish off with decapitation using the katana – employing their carefully cultivated skill to retain a slither of flesh attaching the Samurai's head to the body, so that it didn't fly away. They thought of everything.

Japanese samurai swords are held in mythical esteem as the finest cutting weapons ever devised and top examples fetch six-figure sums. A 17th century katana by master maker Yamaura Masayuki sold for £265,500 in 1993 and might fetch double if auctioned today. Many blades date back to medieval times but still look good-as-new thanks to a lengthy tempering processes involving fire and water. Experts examine a blade by laying it along the length of the arm and looking for the wavy milky line as the metal catches the light.

SWORD TRADING

There are strict rules on purchase and ownership and it is illegal to trade in many weapons (such as 20th century samurai swords, although a minority are covered by exemption). Don't buy outside of the confines of the law, and only purchase from reputable dealers and auction houses. Touring museums help adventurous investors to develop their tastes and preferences in cold steel. The National Army Museum and the Wallace Collection, both in London, and the Royal Armouries in Leeds, are all good places to start. Traders include Michael German Antiques, www.antiqueweapons.com.

Teddy Bear

The teddy bear is the world's most popular as well as collectable toy. The top values tend to be those made by the German toy company Steiff. The company began making cuddly toys after Richard Steiff saw performing bears at the circus in 1902. The term *teddy* was coined in the same year. It came into being when an American newspaper cartoon popularised a recent incident of President Theodore "Teddy" Roosevelt declining to shoot a bound and manacled wild bear. A shop took up the idea and made "Teddy's bear", or teddy bears, as an ornament and plaything.

The record paid for a Steiff is £110,000 in 1994, for a 1905 Teddy Girl.

Others include £101,556 for a 1926 Happy in 2002 and £82,000 paid in 2000 for the oldest Steiff bear thought to exist – a PB28 made in 1904 – just a year after the company was founded. An original black mourning Steiff bear produced in 1912 to commemorate the sinking of the Titanic sold for £91,750 in 2000, while even a modern reproduction can change hands for £500.

Bears made between the Twenties and Thirties can fetch up to £1000 while those produced in the Forties and Fifties tend to fetch far less, and rarely top £100.

Modern "limited edition" Steiffs can also be collectable.

Provenance is key, with proof, such as authentic photos and past owner verification, usually at least doubling the value. Condition for the older bears almost counts for as much as a maker's label; a smart investment becomes a tatty buy if the stuffing is falling out.

Features such as unusual colours and designs among teddies are also important for vintage bears.

As a rule it is the oldest teddies, well-preserved, that command the high demand among investors. This is simply because few of such bears have not lost their looks over time, after years of rough loving care from child owners. And a lovely but tatty bear with however much history in the world is nought but a forlorn creature in the investment world. Their value exists only through cherished memories, so keep such specimens for cuddles rather than cash.

 ALOYSIUS REVISITED

Brideshead Revisited, the 1981 TV series based on the book by Evelyn Waugh, played an important role in transforming a childhood toy into a modern collectable. The character Sebastian Flyte famously spent much of his time with teddy bear Aloysius. Aloysius now lives at the Teddy Bears of Witney shop and museum, a dozen miles away from the Oxford where Sebastian dragged him around. He is worth at least £25,000 and was made in 1907 by Ideal Toy Company in America.

Teddy bears that do not hold the Steiff label can still hold value if particularly unusual and dressed in designer clothes. The record price paid for a teddy is £130,000 for a Louis Vuitton dressed bear in 2000.

Other German bear-makers that are collectable include those of Schuco, Bing and Gebrüder Sussenguth, the last of which made Peter Bears.

Peter Bears were realistic, with dangerous looking teeth. Unfortunately this frightened off children so production stopped pretty promptly, and there are now just a few survivors left.

English makers also have collectable cachet, and those to look out for include any manufactured by Farnell, Chad Valley, Chiltern and Merrythought.

JOIN THE PICNIC

National and regional auctions of toys and dolls are a good source for teddies as are the London International Antique and Artists Dolls, Toys, Miniatures, Teddy Bears and Vintage Fashion Fairs (www.grannysgoodiesfairs.com). See online magazine www.teddybear-news.info.

Tin Robots

Tin robots were born out of the defeat of Japan in World War II. Broken and humiliated under American occupation, the Japanese looked to a far-flung science fiction future for escape. One of the most significant ways they went about this was by making toy robots and rockets from old recycled tin.

Wind up and battery-operated models with brightly coloured decorations and futuristic designs of the era were necessarily cheap for the shattered economy. But in recent years enthusiasts have grown to appreciate their quirky appeal. Names such as Lavender fat-boy, Mr Atomic and Smoking Spaceman are among the huge range of collectable robots produced by the Japanese during the Fifties and Sixties, which now sell for hundreds or even thousands of pounds.

The world record is £20,565 paid in 2001 for an extremely rare original tin robot called Machine Man, made in 1958 by Japanese maker Masudaya.

The Japanese first started manufacturing robots as a cottage industry, and the origins of many early models are not known. For collectors, colour, quality, rarity and mechanical complexity are as much interest as a manufacturer's label.

The most successful of the Japanese toymakers was Horikawa – whose products bear an SH stamp – which was founded in Tokyo in 1959. Masudaya models are recognised by a TM stamp. Others include "Alps", and Yonezawa that used a Y.

Among the most bizarre are a Mr Chief smoking robot made in 1965 by Yoshiya, which puffs out smoke from its head and can now fetch as much as £900.

Other multi-skilled robots include the Attacking Martian by Horikawa from the early Sixties. The robot would stroll along swinging his arms, occasionally opening up a green-eyed chest to reveal an arsenal of shooting guns. This Attacking Martian toy robot can fetch £500, while even an early Eighties re-issue may go for £150.

Robbie the Robot, who starred in the 1956 Hollywood movie *Forbidden Planet*, is the most iconic robot design and widely copied in Japanese robot toys.

A 1950s Revolving Flashing Robot by Alps is one of the most valuable imitations and collectors can pay up to £2500 if it still has the original box. Another good copy is the clockwork Action Planet Robot made by Yoshiya in 1958 with a sparking head. This can change hands for £400.

The real Robbie was more than seven feet tall and cost $125,000 to make. He was inducted into the Robot Hall of Fame in 2004 and is now a priceless icon.

THREE LAWS OF ROBOTICS

There are Three Laws of Robotics as stated by author Isaac Asimov. 1. A robot may not injure a human being or allow one to come to harm. 2. A robot must obey orders given by a human unless it conflicts against the first law. 3. A robot must protect its own existence, as long as this does not conflict with the first or second law. If these rules are followed you have a safe investment.

As with other collectable toys, condition is key when looking to buy. Tin robots are particularly susceptible to scratches to transfers, splits in the metal and even rust. An original box will bump up the value hugely, as packaging designs can be colourful and few have survived the ravages of time.

Larger sized robots more than ten inches tall are also among the most sought after, as are those bigger ones made of metal rather than plastic, which took over in the Sixties.

Robots that provide windows to show how mechanics operate – whether by battery or windup – are also seen as particularly appealing among collectors.

ROBO RESEARCH

Research is a major part of the appeal to this fascinating market. Books include *Robots: Spaceships and Other Tin Toys*, by Teruhisa Kitahara. For trading information check out the Robot Japan website links page: www.robot-japan.com/links.asp.

Titanic

'Be British, boys, be British,' shouted Captain Edward John Smith.

Some gentlemen went downstairs, after putting loved ones on a lifeboat, to don their tuxedos. They returned to the deck to enjoy a final cigar. And, of course, the band played on, the ship sank, and the men were stoic, brave, gentlemanly – British, or the old kind of British anyway, to the end.

The luxury liner struck an iceberg just before midnight on April 14, 1912. Two hours and forty minutes later at 2.20am it sank. Of the 2223 passengers and crew that left Southampton on the voyage to America, 1517 died in the freezing Atlantic. The Titanic had a lifeboat capacity of 1178.

Anything relating to the Titanic is of collectable value but it is those artefacts that portray something of the human drama that tend to be most sought after.

The highest price paid to date is £90,000 in 2007 for what many believe was the key that could have saved the Titanic. It belonged to the original second officer David Blair and may have opened a lock in the crow's nest where the binoculars were kept.

Blair was bumped off the maiden voyage at the last minute and forgot to hand over the keys to his replacement. Without them, vital minutes may have been lost as lookouts searched for icebergs with naked eyes rather than binoculars.

Previously the record was £58,000 paid in 2006 for a miniature of Mary Churchill Hungerford, mother of American first class passenger and author Helen Churchill Candee. The portrait was handed to passenger Edward Kent for safekeeping in a harrowing well-documented episode as she got into the lifeboat. It was later recovered from his corpse.

A Titanic passenger's gold-plated watch, the hands of which remained at 2.21am (the time when the vessel finally disappeared) fetched £19,800 in 2002. The same watch might have fetched £2000, as did many others, just a decade earlier.

WOMEN AND CHILDREN FIRST, MONEY SECOND

Women and children first, typically followed by those with money. The Titanic survival rate was 60% for first class ticket holders, 44% for second class and 25% for third class passengers. Only 24% of crew survived.

The 1997 film *Titanic*, starring Kate Winslet and Leonardo DiCaprio, has also had a major impact in boosting interest – and values – in recent years, by adding romance to the appeal.

Letters are particularly sought after due to their historic account of the traumatic events and have sold for up to £40,000. Before the movie they went for less than £10,000.

A canvas sack in which a drowned victim's possessions were sent home to England after being discovered off the coast of Canada can sell for £15,000.

Authentic artefacts with the Titanic insignia, which includes the White Star Line logo, are also extremely collectable. They fetch anything from £10,000 for a menu card to less than £1000 for a Turkish-bath ticket stub.

The holy grail of Titanic mythology is the final ship's log entry by Captain Smith, which has so far not been recovered.

A Titanic biscuit bearing the ship's image has sold for £3525.

The last surviving passenger of the Titanic, Millvina Dean, was a nine-week old baby when lowered in a wicker basket into the lifeboat number 13. She died aged 97 in May 2009.

NAVIGATE WITH CARE

The market is flooded with fakes so don't buy without expert verification. Check out the British Titanic Society at www.britishtitanicsociety.com, and Henry Aldridge & Son (www.henry-aldridge.co.uk).

Top Hats

The first top hat was worn by haberdasher John Hetherington in 1797 and its appearance caused a riot – according to a 19th century story. 'Several women fainted, children screamed, dogs yelped, and an errand boy's arm was broken when he was trampled by the mob,' claimed officers of the Crown. The fashion offender was told if he breached the peace again he would face a £500 penalty.

But by 1850 even Prince Albert was wearing a topper and no gentlemen – rich or poor, and no matter his class – would venture out without wearing his top hat. But in the early 20th century the topper had become reserved for special occasions and only the wealthy dandy was still wearing it as a fashion accessory.

It is the high-class top hats made of woven silk that tend to be the most collectable today and the most impressive examples can fetch as much as £5000. And with gentleman enthusiasts awakened to the exclusive cachet of the silk hat, prices have risen by as much as 50% over the past five years, with a scramble to ensure everyone looks the best at the races.

The price hike has come about because the original French silk loom used for making top hats was destroyed in the Sixties, when the Lyon-based brothers that owned the machinery had a violent disagreement and it was thrown in the River Seine.

Big heads can be blamed for the highest prices as sizes that are popular today were unusually large for the Victorian era, and are accordingly rare. This means the bigger the head the more expensive the investment. Smaller crowns are relatively cheap.

Prices for silk top hats start at about £1000 and a quality example that will fit most heads can be purchased for £2000 to £3000. Anything above this is a bespoke example of the very highest quality.

Hat-makers with pedigree to look out for include Henry Heath of London, Scott & Co, Locke & Co Hatters, and Bates of St James in London.

    IF THE HAT FITS, WEAR IT

What's your hat size? The modern method is simply putting a tape measure around the circumference of the head. The traditional way is to add the length of the skull to the width and divide it by two. A typical hat size is 7 1/8 to 7 1/4 inches.

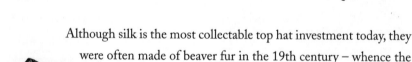

Although silk is the most collectable top hat investment today, they were often made of beaver fur in the 19th century – whence the term "refurbished" originates.

Newly made top hats made of felt or silk-style can still be purchased for less than £200, while vintage examples in need of love might be picked up for £50. When going out, wearing a top hat at night, make sure to follow the gentleman's correct etiquette of matching it with white tie – never black – and evening tails.

Opera top hats are another option and can be folded up and sat upon during a long night at the theatre. Modern ribbed silk opera top hats can be picked up for £150; but be wary of some cheaper satin, as this can be a false economy.

To keep your top hat in fine condition it should regularly be buffed with a velvet pad to help it retain its sheen and stored in a special hat box well away from moths.

GETTING A HEAD START

Top hats pop up in the most curious places. Reputable traders include Hertherington Hats (www.toffs-r-us.com); Hornets in Kensington (www.hornetshats.com); Lock & Co (www.lockhatters.co.uk) and Bates (www.bates-hats.co.uk).

Toy Soldiers

The science fiction author H. G. Wells was one of the first proponents of toy soldiers and wrote a handbook on the subject – the 1913 publication called *Little Wars*. His rules involved careful use of tape measures, the terrain and artillery options for knocking down opponents. Not just males but 'girls of the better sort' and 'rare and gifted women' were also allowed to make the battlefield manoeuvres.

The famous author concluded: 'You have only to play at Little Wars three or four times to realise just what a blundering thing Great War must be.' The very next year the words proved most prophetic.

Although toy soldiers have been around since the time of the Egyptian Pharaohs it wasn't until the late 18th century that they began to be mass-produced.

They were initially made by a Paris-based company called Mignot, and the German George Heyde, the latter using slate – focusing on battle scenes often inspired by the Prussian ruler Frederick the Great.

However, in 1893 William Britain invented the lighter and less costly hollowed out toy soldier that transformed the home market and created a Victorian favourite for British families. It is still an icon today.

"Britains" produced red boxes of toy soldiers endorsed by the Royal Family, whose patriotic and colourful armies were designed to trumpet forth the glories of the Empire. The military figures that were made from the late Victorian era right up until the end of the Fifties are the most prized and can fetch thousands of pounds.

Even the most basic Britains toy soldier sets that sold for four shillings as new in 1893 will go for several hundred pounds today. But find a niche, such as female soldiers, Vikings, Boer War figures or Nazis, and prices can soar. A British Army presentation case from the Thirties, with 275 soldiers inside, can fetch £20,000.

Unusual options are among the most collectable and can command four-figures due to their quirky and unusual nature. For example, a set of 1914 air raid wardens sells for £3000, while a 1950s Bahamas brass band will cost £1000.

One of the most valuable is a "village idiot" created after World War I for a Home Farm Series. The figure was introduced after King George V, inspecting the sets, asked 'Where is the village idiot?' It was soon after withdrawn for being too tasteless.

WE SHALL FIGHT THEM ON THE CARPET

The most famous toy soldier collector was wartime leader Winston Churchill, who in his boyhood amassed a prodigious war machine across his nursery floor. True to Churchill's expectation of American supremacy, though, the most impressive collection of all time probably belongs to the US billionaire and publisher Malcolm Forbes. He had an army of 60,000 toy soldiers, which went under the hammer for £500,000 on his death in 1997.

Toy soldier collecting or investment officially began when lead was banned as too poisonous for toys in 1966. Initially, grown men were often embarrassed about admitting their interest, but as prices have climbed the activity has earned military-esque respect.

The figures themselves can double in value depending on whether they saw much military activity or spent most of their time in service on the shelf. The original box is perhaps the most collectable part of the set of all.

Individual figures are also a good way to start a collection, with those in unusual military occupation, such as polishing a pair of boots or playing the violin, particularly sought after.

Although lead has more intrinsic value in the toy soldier market, the generation that grew up with them is dying out – and plastic military figures are now also growing in popularity.

GOING ON PARADE

See *Collectors Gazette* for toy soldier advice and details of trade fairs and classified adverts. Books worth studying first include *Collecting Toy Soldiers* by James Opie.

Train Sets

Vintage toy train sets are not child's play for collectors, with top examples having seen their value drive full-steam ahead as much as ten-fold since the start of the Eighties.

George Stephenson opened the first steam railway track carrying passengers between Stockton and Darlington in 1825 but it took toy makers until 1893 to agree on a standard track size – after which the train investment market took off.

The first were Gauge 1, with the width between the wheels at 48mm, and Gauge 0 at 37mm. Gauge 1 locomotives were two-feet long and although fantastic fun required lots of space in which to run the tracks.

German maker Marklin is considered the best, and their early engines regularly sell at auction for thousands of pounds. Other great makers included Bing and Carette as well as the British firm Bassett-Lowke. An extremely rare 1906 Marklin Gauge V, big enough for a child to drive, sold for a record £113,750 in 2001 – while even modest Gauge 1 sets can sell for £1000.

Marklin accessories are highly sought after and a stylish Thirties Leipzig station is worth £7500. Others can be picked up for £250. Expect to hand over £13,000 for a 1936 Marklin "Cock o' the North" that cost £1500 in the Eighties.

Hornby trains did not arrive until 1920, but thanks to the anti-German sentiment after the Great War – helped along with logos such as 'British Toys for British Boys' – it was an instant hit.

A Hornby model highly regarded by collectors for interwar nostalgia appeal is the Gauge 0 Princess Elizabeth locomotive. This engine cost five guineas when it rolled out of the station in 1937, but can now sell for more than £3000. However, a more modest outlay of £200 should enable you to get a less illustrious 0 model that has enjoyed a few careful runs around the track.

Manufacturers realised that they could sell more trains if they made the model sets smaller and in 1935 they halved the 0 size to create Gauge 00 at 16.5mm as well. The 00 models tend to be cheaper, with examples available from £50.

ELECTROCUTING PETS

The first electrified toy train sets were introduced in the late 19th century but were still a rarity until the 1920s, when more homes were fitted with electricity. These early years were also fraught with the constant danger of electrocution. Train sets zapped many a pet before transformers were introduced to lower track voltages.

The very earliest 19th century trains were one-off working steam engine toys dubbed "dribblers", and constructed of brass. They burned spirits to boil water for their steam, and would run along the floor rather than a track. Few have survived, but the British firm Mamod has made modern collectable equivalents that can be picked up for less than £200.

Enthusiasts can start with a relatively modest outlay of about £80 for a replica locomotive and carriages by Hornby. These trains may not rise in value but should provide many hours of fun, as well as an ideal taster.

As investments, an original box will more than double the value of a train since so few have survived the excitement of youngsters ripping them open for play. If you really want to make money, do not take it out to enjoy it just yet.

 TRAIN SPOTTING

You don't have to be a train spotting anorak but research is vital. Books include *Collectible Model Trains* by David-Paul Gurney and *Toy Trains: A History* by Pierce Carlson. The magazine *Railway Modeller* provides trade and club information.

Travel Posters

The halcyon days of travel are perfectly captured in vintage travel posters. They hark back to a nostalgic time of wholesome happy families where the sun always shone on holiday and public transport was clean and ran on time. Honest.

Edwardian railway travel posters began the beautifully illustrated propaganda to promote early seaside resorts that were connected by train. Bognor Regis, Weston-super-Mare, Bridlington and Skegness were among the vacation destinations put on the map, and announced to be fit to beat anything Johnny Foreigner might have to offer.

During the interwar years the posters captured the romance of holiday – far removed from the drudgery of daily life – with iconic art deco prints that are still fabulous pieces of art. Key to the appeal is the bright and simple designs, helped by the lithography techniques developed at the end of the 19th century whose vibrant colours and energy suited travel posters.

The most collectable have been more than doubling in value since the Nineties. Great original pieces can still be picked up for a couple of hundred pounds but iconic favourites sell for thousands of pounds.

The "Skegness is So Bracing" poster by John Hassall, depicting a fisherman skipping along the beach, is the most famous of all. First released in 1908 for London and North Eastern Railways it captures a bold sense of fun shared by the best posters of the era. First editions sell for more than £5000 – the original painting is worth at least £30,000.

The advertisement was a huge success for the resort and inspired other railways and towns to jump on the poster bandwagon.

The Twenties heralded the golden age of bus and rail travel posters as a powerful marketing tool before package holidays and mass ownership of cars. Using the romance of travel, artists such as Hassall, plus similar bold designers like Frank Sherwin and Tom Purvis, turned Britain into an idyllic playground.

Great iconic examples such as "Somerset's Family Paradise" (Weston-super-Mare) by Purvis in 1949 can fetch £1000. Another vivid example is "Cornwall" by Ronald Lampitt in 1936, complete with an evocative mosaic style, and selling nowadays for £1500.

Other travel poster artists to look for include Norman Wilkinson, Paul Henry, Dudley Hardy, Austin Cooper, Alan Durman, Edward McKnight Kauffer, Frank Newbould and Frank Mason.

Foreign posters are also popular, with themes and styles available in a variety almost as diverse as the range of countries. Examples capturing the exotic style of the continent fuel the nostalgia value. The French have among the most dramatic art deco images, while Irish travel posters are also always in demand for their homely, rural style.

RULING THE WAVES

Cruise ship liners – just like railway firms and tourist boards – promoted the allure of travel with some fabulous artwork. Bright art deco examples from firms such as Blue Star Line and Cunard sell well. Exotic locations and famous liners, such as Lusitania and Mauritania, will also increase the collectable value.

Nostalgia is the driving force, so seek out images portraying the beauty of a lost childhood location. Beach, wholesome family, golf and rail themes always sell well.

Posters are rare – and valuable – as they were often plastered on train station walls and then covered with other advertisements. Surviving copies with tears or other damage are still collectable but worth far less than pristine examples.

DON'T BID FROM THE DECKCHAIR

Prospective investors should go along to enjoy specialist auctions – but be wary of getting caught out in this burgeoning market. Bid with caution, as prices get inflated; and shop around a variety of private dealerships to compare offers.

Specialist travel poster auctioneers include Onslows Auctioneers (www.onslows.co.uk). Among the major auction houses that regularly hold travel poster events is Christie's (www.christies.com).

Tribal Art

The British Empire provided an exciting opportunity for foreign adventure. Colonial explorers often picked up and traded in tribal art thinking they were merely fascinating souvenirs – not realising they were important works of art.

However, in the past 20 years a growing understanding of their intrinsic value means that the top rare tribal art discoveries have risen more than tenfold in value.

The African subcontinent is the main source for tribal art. The main countries tend to be the Democratic Republic of the Congo, Uganda, Tanzania, Kenya, Malawi, Cameroon, Nigeria and Zulu regions of South Africa.

But other areas across the world, including the Himalayas, Pacific Islands, Timor, southeast Asia and Australia, are also worth exploring for their exciting opportunities. Aboriginal art fetching £1000 five years ago may now sell for £4000 or more.

Prices are as diverse as the rich cultural heritages, with collectables ranging from £200 clay pots to £100,000 holy masks. The most collectable era is typically "pre-contact" 19th or early 20th century, before tourism and outside influences corrupted the art.

Earlier pieces rarely survive as they were often destroyed or have decayed over time.

PABLO PICASSO

Picasso observed African carving in 1907. It transformed his art, as can be seen in the five nudes "Les Demoiselles d'Avignon", whose angled heads look like African masks. It provided a catalyst for the cubist art movement, and original pieces capturing this inspirational essence are among the most sought after.

Masks are probably the most interesting collectables. They were typically worn for ceremonies connected with ancestral worship, rites of passage, or arcane religious beliefs. Good original masks start from about £500 but can sell for £10,000 or more.

African masks are among the best documented, while those from southeast Asia and the Himalayas are more undervalued. The masks often purportedly gave dramatic powers to the wearer and those with "fierce energy" tend to sell the best. And adventurous investors be warned: masks with an eerie realism can paradoxically frighten off investors as unattractive.

Shields are another fascinating area. Other markets include original sculptures, tribal cloths and skirts, chieftain headwear, finely crafted stools, pots and grass baskets.

AN ABOMINABLE INVESTMENT

In 1921, Lieutenant Colonel Charles Kenneth Howard-Bury of the British Army led a Tibetan exploration to pave the way for an Everest expedition. He discovered oversized footprints of an 'abominable snowman'. There have since been a number of sightings but no firm evidence. The closest link may well be an ancient Himalayan tribal mask where you can stare at the "spirit" of a Yeti.

A UNESCO treaty enforced in the 1970s made it illegal to export genuine early tribal works from their country of origin, so the majority of legitimate pieces which come on the market today are from existing private collections.

When dealing with tribal art always make sure that what you are doing is legal. After this, provenance, beauty, age, rarity and condition are the key markers for investors.

As an investment, tribal art should be considered as a long-term commitment and collectors should usually hang on to items for at least a decade to expect substantial returns.

 DANCE TO THE AUTHENTIC BEAT

The African tribal market is riddled with fakes – especially as pieces tend not to be from known artists. Provenance is therefore vital. Do plenty of homework and go through a reputable auction house or dealer. Sources of information include Tribal Art magazine (www.tribalartmagazine.com). Traders include Tribal Gathering at www.tribalgatheringlondon.com. See also Clive Loveless' Primal Art (020 8969 5831).

Truffles

Do you go crazy for the scent of rutting wild boars? Then perhaps it is time to invest in the magical underground mushroom fungus known as the truffle.

The truffle enjoys an enigmatic and bewitching flavour all of its own – and contains alpha-androsterol, which is a compound found in the saliva of rutting boars. This not only lowers the sexual inhibitions of sows but also, according to adventurous scientists, can have similar aphrodisiac effects on women.

The most desirable species are the white Alba Truffle (Tuber magnatum), and the Black Périgord (Tuber melanosporum – also known as the black diamond).

These gastronomic delights have seen their prices as much as triple since the new millennium. This boom comes from a combination of growing demand for truffles to eat, along with some dreadful growing weather which has hit supplies hard.

Truffles can fetch as much as £5000 a kilogram – but the typical price tends to be about £300 a kilogram. Occasional auction frenzy has created some incredible record prices. A 1.5kg white truffle sold for £161,000 at a charity auction in 2007, while an 850g piece (about the size of a large potato) went for £28,000 in 2004.

TRUFFLE TRIFLE

The most expensive dessert in the world, being dished out to discerning New York diners in 2007, was a $25,000 chocolate and cream trifle. The magic ingredient was a sprinkling of truffles and gold on top.

Together, the Alba – sometimes also known as the Piedmont after the region of Italy where it can be found – and the Périgord, offer the benchmark of taste quality and investment appeal, but are notoriously hard to farm and discover. Italy, Slovenia and Croatia are home to both types of truffle, while France, Portugal, Spain and Serbia are home to the so-called black diamond Périgold.

They grow by the roots of certain oaks, limes, hazels and occasional pines and cannot be seen – but give off a scent too subtle for human noses.

White truffles are impossible to farm-grow, while growing black ones requires decades of patience and luck as they usually come from transplanted oak seedlings or saplings from trees where truffles were once found.

SNUFFLING FOR TRUFFLES

Although a pig can sniff out truffles they are liable to eat their find so specially trained truffle dogs – worth at least £2000 – are typically used to find the fungus.

Truffle-hunting in Britain has a long history, and is presently enjoying a resurgence thanks to soaring prices. There are more than 70 species of underground fungi but only a few are edible. Perhaps the best is the Summer Truffle, Tuber aestivum, which although a poor relation of the Périgold still has gastronomic appeal.

For British growers, milder winters, wetter springs and hotter summers suit truffles. The continent has recently suffered from conditions becoming too hot and dry.

The collecting season for white truffles is typically October to December while black truffles may be harvested from November to March.

Before foraging in the forests get your nose in a book on the subject to discover where to start. These include *Black Diamond and Other Truffles* by Jean-Marie Rocchia; and *Collins Mushroom Miscellany* by Patrick Harding.

Typewriters

S weating blood and tears over a literary masterpiece is a tough way to make money. But if you lack talent and time to rattle off a bestseller, consider the value of the typewriter on which the words are created.

With the computer age, most 20th century typewriters have become worthless junk as nobody uses them. However, if you own a particularly unusual or historic early typewriter you could be tapping into a fabulous investment.

One of the earliest and most valuable was created by a Danish pastor called Malling Hansen in 1870. He invented the writing ball typewriter – which looked not unlike a collection of party food cheese-and-pineapple sticks surrounding an orange.

The machine did not sell well, but a century later the innovative design came to be admired and adopted by IBM. Just five years ago examples were fetching £37,000. Since then since prices have risen to as high as £70,000 (though typically less).

Most historically influential of typewriters is the "Sholes & Glidden Type Writer" of 1874. This introduced the QWERTY keyboard. The layout was chosen to deliberately retard typing speed, in order to prevent keys from clashing as the typewriter was tapped. The top line also deliberately held all the keys necessary for salesman to impress customers by typing out TYPEWRITER from one row. This keyboard layout is of course identical to the one in use today.

The Scholes & Glidden machine can fetch many thousands of pounds not least because it was also the blueprint for the first commercially successful typewriter produced by the arms manufacturer Remington.

As popular as typewriters such as the Remington were, though, they were fundamentally flawed as you had to type blind without seeing what was printed. Indeed few of the most valuable typewriters were actually any good, and there are actually still plenty of alternative, later, more useable bargains on the market that can be picked up for just a few pounds.

Typewriters produced by firms such as Hammond, Underwood and Waverley, offer great looking examples. They also benefited from some engineering ingenuity behind the keyboards, which can still be appreciated in the smooth action of surviving examples.

Blickensderfer produced the first portable machine in 1893. Such typewriters were popular during World War I and you can pick up a wartime Corona for less than £100. The tripod on which it was seated costs more than double this price.

 RUDE TECHNOLOGY

The first typewriters weren't produced until the late 19th century and initially flopped as few people wanted to buy them. It was viewed as exceptionally rude not to correspond in all matters via handwritten letter.

Physical appeal is an important consideration. Chances are if you think a machine looks great someone else will too. Many examples were decorative, some with gold and inlaid pearls, and this boosts potential investment value.

If anyone famous has tapped away on the typewriter this also has a huge impact on price. A £60 Fifties gold-plated typewriter used by Ian Fleming to write James Bond books was sold at auction for £45,000 in 1995.

TAP INTO A TYPEWRITER

Study the subject. A great industry guide is *Antique Typewriters and Office Collectables* by Darryl Rehr. Another useful read is *Century of the Typewriter* by Wilfred Beeching. Internet sites such as typewriter.rydia.net and www.yesterdaysoffice.com can also help with forums and trading opportunities.

Vintage Shotguns

The days of big game hunting, when Victorian adventurers roamed the wilds of Africa and India shooting at anything that moved, may well be over – but the guns they used still survive.

The appeal comes from the level of top craftsmanship, particularly during the Edwardian era and between the wars, which has never been bettered. The old British weapons lead the way, with know-how and attention to detail – passed down through the generations – lovingly present in every deadly double-barrel.

Over the past couple of decades the value of top collectable firearms has doubled in value. This has been fuelled by the growing popularity of clay pigeon shooting, and the expansion of game-shooting outside the old preserve of landed gentry.

Quality vintage guns cost anything between £5000 and £50,000, while a flood of modern budget-priced guns has also kept the price of cheaper vintage firearms down to fit £1000 budgets.

Most famous is London-based outfit James Purdey & Sons, established in 1814. It received a Royal Warrant in 1868 from the Prince of Wales and even Queen Victoria was a fan, owning a pair of Purdey pistols.

Investors keen to own a piece of Purdey can spend as little as £5000 for a fine example. However, invest £15,000 or more and you are rewarded with exquisite craftsmanship investors find irresistible.

Another highly skilled London bespoke gun manufacturer is Holland & Holland, established in 1835. Boss & Co Gunmakers, established in 1812, meanwhile boasts to be 'builders of best guns only'.

Before balking at the cost, look at the man-hours spent making a handcrafted gun. Top gun-makers charge £70,000 for a bespoke gun but spend up to a thousand hours of skilled workmanship, and up to two years doing the work.

Other lesser but still highly skilled British gun makers include Stephen Grant, Joseph Lang, Henry Atkin and William Evans. Foreign makers with pedigree include Beretta, Browning, Perazzi, Miroku and AyA.

AMERICAN BORES

The vast majority of sports guns are 12-bore. It refers to the amount of lead required to make a round ball that would fit the barrel – not the dimensions of lead shot in a cartridge. A 12-bore is a twelfth of a pound. Smaller 20-bore sports guns are increasingly collectable and favoured by women and Americans.

The detail and balance of a top gun can only be appreciated by holding it. This is why enthusiasts compare a gun's handling and curves to an elegant woman or a thoroughbred horse.

The "side-by-side" is the traditional game gun design where cartridges are fired from two barrels that sit next to each other. In recent years the "over & under" has attracted increased attention because it is favoured by clay pigeon shooters.

The "sidelock" style refers to the way the firing mechanism is installed under plates and curves into the side of the stock. It has been around for more than a century and regarded as the most collectable.

The "boxlock" is another traditional favourite – fitting as a unit within the gun – but, although commonly used on firearms today, it is generally regarded as inferior.

Although British gun craft is the best, for engraving quality the Italians are breathtaking. Master gun engraver Galeazzi provides countryside and hunting scenes, etched in magnificent detail upon the firearms themselves – works of art as much as the guns. His decorations on weapons made by local makers such as Luciano Bosis and Abbiatico & Salvinelli can go for £20,000 or more.

 ## LICENSE TO MAKE A KILLING

It is essential to try your luck at clay pigeon shooting first, where you can be measured up for a suitable gun. Local gun shops can also be a great help. Firearm owners must have a shotgun certificate, which costs £50.

Check out the Clay Pigeon Shooting Association (www.cpsa.co.uk) and the British Association for Shooting and Conservation (www.basc.org.uk). See also *Vintage Guns for the Modern Shot* by Diggory Hadoke. Gun auctioneers include Christie's, Bonhams, Gavin Gardiner and Holt's. Magazines include *Shooting Times, Sporting Shooter, Shooting Gazette.*

Vinyl Records

T he death of vinyl was announced prematurely in the Eighties when compact discs arrived. At the time CDs, and then later MP3 formats, seemed more convenient and exciting.

But in recent years many music lovers have come back to the more lasting and undoubtedly better sounding tones of records. Vinyl has turned favourite music into a sound investment. Records that were thrown away as junk or sold in bargain bins and charity shops a couple of decades ago are now fetching hundreds or even thousands of pounds.

The perennial top investments are the bands with international appeal that have stood the test of time. At the head is The Beatles. Others include The Rolling Stones, Pink Floyd, The Who, Queen and The Smiths.

For individuals Elvis Presley, David Bowie, Bob Dylan, Jimi Hendrix, Cliff Richard, Elton John and Marc Bolan are among the most sought after.

Industry magazine *Record Collector* puts The Beatles' first numbered White Album as top for rarity value, with a conservative estimate of up to £7000 for one of the first ten copies – though investors might pay twice that amount.

Other rarities include a swearing Marc Bolan on a Hard on Love acetate plus the silk-sleeve padded Rolling Stones album Their Satanic Majesties Request, both worth £2000.

John Lennon & Yoko Ono's experimental 1968 album, featuring the couple nude on the cover, is worth £3000 for a mono version – rarity rather than musical appeal pushing up its price.

THE QUARRY MEN

The most coveted is a seven-inch single "That'll Be the Day", recorded by the Quarry Men in 1958 before they were renamed The Beatles. There is only one copy in existence and it is owned by Sir Paul McCartney. It was cut in a booth on acetate 78rpm. It is worth at least £100,000 – though might sell for far more.

First pressings are usually the most valuable, as they were often produced in a small number before the record was a hit. Early demos and limited exports are also highly sought after among die-hard collectors. The record company and issue code on the disc and sleeve can help reveal the identity.

Other considerations include whether it was a commercial or promotional release, recorded in stereo or mono, included any freebies, or has a picture sleeve. The fact it is a single, album or extended player is not the most important consideration – it is the collectable cachet that matters.

Condition is also paramount. A mint condition is worth twice that of a "very good" example, with a few minor scuffs and surface scratches. Anything less is not usually considered as collectable – a badly scratched copy could fetch less than a tenth of its best value.

Although the big names have seen some of the most impressive rises in price in recent years, there is also a growing market for their more obscure or early recordings – even though this may not be their best music.

An early Elton John disc recorded in the late Sixties, when he was known as Reg Dwight, might go for £600. An early "U2: Three" 12" single from 1981 signed by Bono has a valuation of £3000.

MAKING MUSIC MAKE MONEY

Internet trading has transformed the market, but for many vinyl investors there is no substitute for the added fun of rummaging through racks at specialist record shops or trade fairs.

Befriending the dealer at your local second-hand record store can also prove invaluable. But those wishing to sell must realise traders typically offer half the price at which they wish to sell.

An excellent source of information with details of shops and fairs is the magazine *Record Collector*. It also publishes the industry bible *Rare Record Price Guide* each year – though prices are often conservative. For American releases, investors can check out *Goldmine Record Album Price Guide* and *Goldmine Price Guide to 45rpm Records*.

Walking Sticks

The walking stick is a gentleman's fashion accessory, not just an aid to the elderly or infirm. In its Victorian and Edwardian heyday it was a vital accoutrement for swaggering, pointing, flirting, commanding and waving about on street corners.

The decorative handles are what makes most of them collectable – some soaring up to three-times in value over the past 20 years. These used to be chosen before the stick, which was usually made of the flexible bamboo malacca.

The stick-swishing adventurer might have a dozen canes from which to choose, including wooden favourites for city strolls, black with silver handle for evening wear and rustics for weekend country rambles.

Decorative handles tended to be in wood, silver, ivory, ebony or porcelain inspired by elaborate animal figures as well as a wide range of country sports, and collectable artistic and erotic figurines. Carved dog heads were a favourite for handles, while cats were deemed vermin so were less abundant – the more rare cat ones can cost more than five times as much today and might fetch £400.

The Victorian fascination with nature extends to stick construction. Ivory is particularly sought after – especially carved in the Orient – and exotically carved handles can fetch £800 to £4000. If the stick is also carved then prices soar far higher.

Marine life also held great interest in the 19th century and walking sticks made of whale bone, shark or with walrus tusk can command prices of £500. Wooden Victorian folk art sticks can be found for between £100 and £200.

BULLSTICK

The penis of a bull – or pizzle – was a favourite among both Victorian gentlemen and ladies taking a stroll. Stretched around a thin metal rod it could extend to a typical 36 inches in length. Examples can be bought for about £200.

The "system" gadget walking stick is the most valuable. Among the most rare is a hidden violin cane, with a bow safely stored in its shaft, used by street performers and now worth £10,000. Other hidden walking stick instruments include flutes, horns and conductor's batons.

Other collectable walking sticks include those with hidden ear trumpets, worth £5000, swords and guns (illegal to carry today), brollies, fishing rods, telescopes, compasses and cigarette lighters.

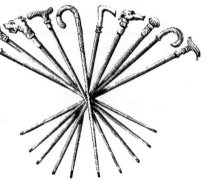

Early doctors had pomanders kept in the top of sticks to ward off sickness, which can fetch more than £2000, while city dwellers also had smelling-salt compartments to combat unpleasant odours.

Walking sticks have been around since the origins of mankind – Caine killed his brother Abel with one according to the Bible. But the first findings were in the tomb of

Egyptian king Tutankhamun, who reigned between 1333 and 1324 BC, when explorer Howard Carter opened his tomb in 1922 to find 132 sticks.

They started to play a ceremonial role in Britain from the mid-17th century. Typically plainer than later sticks with a long ferrule – tip touching the ground – they can cost £1000.

It wasn't until the 19th century that it became essential to the attire of the Victorian gentleman. This is the most collectable era, with a vast selection of choice that lasts until the outbreak of World War I.

TAKING A STROLL

Saunter along to a specialist dealer such as stick specialist shop Michael German of Kensington, London (www.antiquecanes.com). As well as all the new stylish walking you'll be doing, don't forget to put your feet up with some research, including the booklet *Walking Sticks*, by Catherine Dike.

War Games

War games played in the living room rather than the battlefield can be a great investment. The main appeal is not the game itself – which is usually a rip-off of an already established board game – but the innovative design and ideas that turned it into a morale-boosting diversion in wartime. These games are not only tremendous nostalgic fun but are a fascinating piece of history that continues to rise in value.

 "OLD BILL'S RACE"

The First World War provided the greatest propaganda forum for war games. In 1914 a "Recruiting for Kitchener's Army" game went around the country in search of able-bodied recruits. Drink, smoking and defective teeth knocked you back on the board, while the winner was the player that got the most recruits who had 'signed the pledge'. By 1917 we had a game called Old Bill's Race – focusing on pushing on to Berlin. Hazards to avoid included 'Gassed – go to ambulance' and 'Killed – back to base'. Old Bill's Race can still be picked up for £250 and Kitchener's Army for about £100.

World War II is the most collectable era as this marked a high point for board and card games before the arrival of television broke up the family fun.

Moral outrage transformed innocent games, such as Snakes and Ladders, into propaganda with the same rules but different objectives. For example, British bombing game Target for Tonight had searchlights acting as snakes as you tried to reach Berlin. It can now sell for more than £200.

Another popular diversion was an anti-Hitler game resembling tiddlywinks called V Game, where the German ruler was the bull's eye target to be hit with a "V1 bomb". It can fetch £800.

It is important for investors not to be offended by some of their more politically incorrect rules – which can involve, as above, scoring points by bombing cities – but to appreciate them in the context of their era.

One of the most valuable is a German-manufactured 1940 game called Bomber Über England. It is extremely rare and good examples have gone for £2600. It was a copy of the game bagatelle, only using a map of Blighty for target practice.

Not all war board games involve killing the enemy. Black-Out involves marching through the streets of London late at night ordering residents to turn off their lights. The game originally cost just two shillings but might now fetch £600.

Other fabulous board games from World War II that change hands for hundreds of pounds include Raiders And Fighters, Pinpoint the Bomber, and Aviation – the Aerial Tactics Game of Attack and Defence.

War card games are also collectable. These include Top Trumps-style England Expects and a Happy Family derivative called Victory, with the Home Front, Hitler and his cronies, and the army among the sets to collect. These are now sold for less than £100.

And these old amusements don't even have to have a war theme for them to be a collectable war game. Conventional board games such as Monopoly had spinning cards rather than dice during WWII, because of rationing, making such war-versions more valuable.

As with most alternative investments, condition is key. However, because of the rarity and unusual nature of war board games, the most rare games can still command a strong price even if a box is tatty – just as long as it is a complete set.

WHO DARES WINS

Turn off the telly and bring out the slippers. There is no point getting involved unless you can appreciate the appeal by playing games yourself. Modern derivatives, such as "Escape From Colditz", are great places to kick-start an interest. Rarity means condition is not so important – just so long as games are complete. Don't let potential purchases slip away but snap them up. *The Home Front: British Wartime Memorabilia 1939-1945* and *Tommy's War*, by Peter Doyle and Paul Evans, offer information, while *Antiques Trade Gazette* (www.antiquestradegazette.com), provides price guides and market sales.

Watches

The wristwatch has been the timekeeper of choice ever since World War I, when soldiers realised that glancing at a wrist was better than fumbling for a pocket watch. Before that (from about 1650) any self-respecting gentleman adventurer had much preferred the habit of whisking out a fob watch if they had wanted to check if it was time for tiffin.

The values for top luxury watches have soared over the past three decades and iconic status symbols like Rolex, Patek Philippe and Cartier now sell for thousands of pounds. But these are not just baubles for the super-rich. As adventurous investments, the quality examples have more than doubled in value since the millennium and are now always in demand.

Those who wish to tell the time on a tighter budget can still enjoy the investment with cheaper bets, with Swatches, retros and digital watches also leaping in price.

 ## SPLASH ON A ROLEX

In the true spirit of adventure, Englishwoman Mercedes Gleitz became the first woman to swim the English Channel in 1927. On the swim she wore the first practical waterproof watch, the Rolex Oyster, to test out its durability. The advertising proved a great success and helped turn the watch into a classic.

The top price paid for a wristwatch is £2.6m for a 1929 World Time Patek in platinum, sold in 2002. Several others have sold for more than £1m.

Patek Philippe's platinum 10-day power reserve model introduced to celebrate the millennium cost £20,000 new but can now change hands for £30,000. The Rolex is a relative snip with the most ever paid for a vintage Rolex being £209,520 for a 1953 triple calendar model in 2004.

The best-known Rolex classic is the Daytona Chronograph with Paul Newman dial. Costing £2000 in the Eighties it can now sell for as much as £30,000. The Rolex Oyster Perpetual Submariner was introduced in 1954. Recent second-hand Submariner examples can go for less than £3000 – though you can pay far more.

Cartier is not so renowned for its skills but makes up for any shortcomings with style.

Other luxury classic makers worth looking at include Vacheron Constantin, Breguet and Panerai. Breitlings, Heuers, Longines and Omega may also be worth a punt.

Swatch began in the early Eighties as a cheap but reliable plastic watch that soon turned into a fashion accessory. New Swatches start at £30 but look for early limited "specials" designed by artists for top prices. Among the most valuable is a 1985 Kiki Picasso by Christian Chapiron worth at least £15,000.

The first digital watches came out in the early Seventies with red-glowing light emitting diodes and, to save energy, buttons that had to be pressed to read the time. Early classics made by Bulova and Commodore can still be picked up for between £100 and £200.

Futuristic eye-catching dial designs by competitors were introduced to seize the momentum from the digital revolution, and some, such as the Spaceman Audacieuse, now sell at auction for more than £300.

Don't buy anything damaged or in poor working order. Seek out the provenance. Rolex has a reference number on every watch, so it should be easy to check on these details. Patek can trace cases, movement numbers and see if the watch has been restored by one of its specialists.

Chronograph extras are always very popular, with working buttons, dials, time zones, waterproof details and adventure information boosting values.

Horological auctions can provide bargains, with unsold stock or classics available that have slipped through the net. Items typically cost more in a specialist shop.

FIND THE RIGHT TIME

Check out watch magazines such as *QP* (www.qpmagazine.com). The world's leading watch auction house is Antiquorum in Geneva (www.antiquorum.com). Expert advice can be had from the British Horological Institute (www.bhi.co.uk).

Web Domain Names

Trading in domain names – the web jargon for internet website addresses – has been one of the new industries of the 21st century. The domain is the title immediately following the world wide web (www) letters, and also includes the chosen suffix such as .com or .co.uk. It can be used for creating new email addresses, too.

The snappiest names are usually purchased from investors who have already registered the domains and are willing to sell their rights for a profit. These names can be found by trawling through the specialist domain traders, with independent sellers able to use the facility for a fee of typically £5 a year.

Once a domain name has been registered it can be kept in mothballs or housed with a hosting company and turned into a website. Traders and ISPs (internet service providers) may offer free parking for a website or, if you are unfortunate, may charge as much as £50 a year for the privilege. The art of sitting on a domain name in the hope that it might one day strike gold is known as cyber-squatting.

You are never able to purchase a domain name outright, but only lease it for between two and ten years. Costs typically start at £5 a year but can be far higher. The person with the right has first option for renewal.

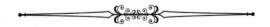

There are few original opportunities in the .co.uk and .com market, but plenty with unusual suffixes such as .eu, .biz, .pro, .info and .tv, or those from countries with small populations but useful web-abbreviated endings (such as .to or Tongo).

The blue-chip cachet of .com and co.uk means these will always be in most demand and the most bankable – but they also command the top premium prices.

With up to 69 letters allowed on an individual domain, investors are only limited by their imagination. Although generic terms are okay, if you register a famous name as a domain you could also run into trouble when trading it, unless it can be proved you are not making money out of the website.

WORLD RECORD

The world record paid for a domain name is the £4.7m paid for business.com at the height of the dotcom boom in the early noughties.

Surf the net and window shop through the wide range of domain-traders to get an idea of the huge scale of prices – from less than £5 to more than £1m. Many domain owners are also willing to auction off their names in search of the best price; a high-risk gamble for sellers, but a great place to find bargains.

www.tobywalne.co.uk

Check to make sure that the domain-trader offers free parking for your website – go elsewhere if they charge for the privilege. Traders typically make their money by providing space for a potential website and then offering design assistance.

Extra charges on top of a typical yearly rental fee include a one-off registration fee and possible exit penalties if you wish someone to look after your domain name at a later date.

MAKING A NAME FOR YOURSELF ONLINE

Nominet UK registers .uk names and offers help (www.nominet.org.uk). The Internet Corporation for Assigned Names and Numbers (ICANN) is the governing body (www.icann.org). The Internet Assigned Numbers Authority offers domain registration guidance at www.iana.org. Domain name traders include www.easyspace.com.

Wedgwood Pottery

Wedgwood was founded in 1759 by Josiah Wedgwood. Inspired by the fine bone china of the Orient, he decided to make his own quality earthenware. It was so good that by 1765 Queen Charlotte, wife of King George III, was buying it.

As potter to Her Majesty he provided cream "Queen's Ware" and powder blue and classic white relief "Jasper Ware", which was so dense it did not need glazing. Another 18th century classic was "Black Basalt".

His early ornamentals are also collectable – items such as vases, candlesticks and decorative pots, which Wedgwood made between 1769 and 1780, when he teamed up with another master potter of the era Thomas Bentley.

Prices vary hugely depending on individual tastes, but any chips or cracks in whatever item you purchase can instantly turn a unique treasure into worthless junk.

Westwood medallions and plaques of the 18th century are incredibly detailed. Four oval plaques embossed with Greek classical figures might sell at auction for £2000 while a larger single medallion of George III has gone for £3000.

A pair of 1780 encaustic vases recently went for a smashing £5500, but a Wedgwood plaque of Medusa from the same era might do well to shift for £650. The practical beauty of tableware is hardest to put a price on as tastes vary so much.

The company was rocked by a huge forgery scandal in 1994, when the market was flooded with fakes. Even the Wedgwood Museum was found to possess 50 high-class copies produced by a local potter. Seek expert help before buying.

Wedgwood was renamed Waterford Wedgwood after it snapped up Waterford Crystal in 1986. It has also incorporated Coalport and Mason's Ironstone in recent years.

In the late Nineties Wedgwood purchased Rosenthal and more recently also acquired Royal Doulton. It went into receivership at the start of 2009 but was later picked up by an American equity firm. The future remains uncertain, but investments remain safe and very worthwhile.

 ## 21ˢᵗ CENTURY CRISIS

The 21st century crisis facing Wedgwood and other great British pottery firms is due to a slump in demand for modern pottery but this has little impact on the collectable market, which tends to focus mostly on 18th century items.

Royal Worcester and Spode are other great potters recently smashed by the recession but still highly collectable. The historic companies merged in 2006 and were forced into administration at the end of 2008.

Royal Worcester was founded in 1751 by Dr John Wall and partners during the reign of King George II. As a maker of elegant porcelain teaware, it received a royal warrant in 1789.

Early examples are famed for ornate shapes and patterns, often decorated with vivid colours. 18th century examples made at the Dr Wall factory go from a few hundred pounds to priceless. An early 20th century Royal Worcester plaque fetched £6500 in 2008, while teaware can go for hundreds of pounds.

Spode was set up in Stoke-on-Trent in 1767 by Josiah Spode, who transformed the industry. He made his name for the perfection of under glaze blue printing in 1784. But in the 1790s Spode made the most incredible discovery of all, with the perfection of fine bone china.

Early examples of the most finely decorated Spode can go for more than £1000, while 19th century earthenware examples can be picked up for £100 (though usually they fetch more).

  ## PUTTING THE PIECES TOGETHER

Prospective buyers should seek expert advice and do their homework first by studying books, as there are such a variety of designs and qualities, as well as a fascinating history behind it all. *Miller's Ceramics Buyer's Guide* by John Sandon is a good starting point. See also the Wedgwood Visitor Centre and Museum, Stoke-on-Trent (www.wedgwoodvisitorcentre.com and www.wedgwoodmuseum.org.uk). The Worcester Museum (www.worcesterporcelainmuseum.org.uk) and Spode Museum Trust (www.spode.co.uk) are also worth a look.

Wine

R aise a glass to a fine wine investment where even losers can celebrate. Pick a vintage winner and heady returns that double in value over five years are quite possible; while if it fails to live up to expectation you can simply drown your sorrows in style.

France is the best place for investing in wine. The most famous Bordeaux red wines, known as clarets, tend to be the best bets for the British market.

The biggest guns to look out for are the five first growths – Premier Crus – of Haut-Brion, Lafite-Rothschild, Latour, Margaux and Mouton Rothschild. These are deemed to be the best blue-chip names for investing, along with Cheval Blanc, Ausone and Pétrus.

The year the wine was produced plays a crucial factor in values, as the weather dictates the final quality of wine. Classic Bordeaux past vintages include 1982, 1989, 1990, 1995, 1996, 2000, 2003 and 2005.

One of the biggest winners in recent years is Lafite-Rothschild '82. A 12-bottle crate purchased for £275 when it first hit the wine racks can fetch as much as £25,000 on the market today.

Shrewd investors can also look at the second tier of "super-seconds" that includes Pichon-Lalande, Léoville-Las Cases, Cos d'Estournel, Lafleur, Montrose, Léoville-Barton, Palmer and Lynch-Bages.

The best way to boost profits is the high risk of buying the wine before it is even bottled – *en primeur* – in spring, when an army of wine critics and merchants descend on Bordeaux in March and April for sampling.

Another tip is to second-guess international market demand. In the past decade, annual wine consumption has doubled to 30 bottles per person in Britain. Rich wine buyers from Russia and China have also been bidding for the top vintages in the wine market.

 ## GRAPE EXPECTATIONS

No matter what you or other tasters think, it is American wine connoisseur Robert Parker who calls the shots. His tongue most affects the value of wines. Parker marks everything he sips out of 100. Anything over 96 is classed as 'an extraordinary wine' and turns a fine drink into a superb investment winner. *The Wine Advocate* magazine also has a huge impact on values.

As an investment the wine should be stored in a bonded warehouse, ensuring that no VAT or duty will be paid on your wine until or unless released. The wine can avoid tax when traded if it remains bonded.

The taxman also regards wine as a 'wasting asset', so is not normally liable for capital gains tax unless it has been collecting dust for at least 50 years.

Being bonded, the buyers should also get a certificate of ownership, offering proof of history when traded later on. Bonded warehouses will store the wine safely in dark and cold areas, which are temperature-controlled and free from any vibrations.

A top wine should typically be stored at least 10 years as an investment opportunity, although jumps in the market may mean trading within a year is an option. Most wines are made to be drunk within a few years but if you buy the very best – particularly if in big magnum or double magnum bottles – there is no reason why your investment shouldn't last 40 years.

Storing wine under bond will typically cost £5 to £15 per case a year, and this should include insurance against loss or damage. A fine wine can be ruined if stored in the fluctuating atmosphere of a kitchen or living room – it also offers the perilous temptation of uncorking it.

When it is time to sell, the typical option is to sell it back to the merchant, but they can take a 10% cut of its market value. If you sell through auction houses they will also demand a seller's premium of about 10 to 12%.

 DRUNK ON PROFIT

Leading wine merchants include Berry Bros & Rudd, Bibendum, Farr Vintners, Seckford, John Armit and Goedhuis. Unfortunately, the wine investment market is unregulated so check website www.investdrinks.org for traders to avoid.

Woodland

C
an't see the wood for the trees? Then consider investing in a forest, to inspect things at a more leisurely pace. Woodland offers a straightforward and environmentally friendly way to grow money, with some great tax-break opportunities.

The price of timber in Britain, along with the forest in which it grows, has together typically doubled in value over the past five years. And for those investors who opt for commercial forestry, woodland is sold income tax free, avoids capital gains tax, and even escapes inheritance tax.

However, it is not an investment for the fainthearted. The minimum outlay is typically £10,000 and investors should expect to hold on to their trees for at least a decade to enjoy healthy financial returns.

Unlike oil and gas, woodland is a renewable natural resource: when you cut the trees down to sell, you replant for the next generation to grow.

Typical woodland purchases are spruce, with the rural uplands of Scotland, Wales and northern England being prime regions for investment. Prices vary on geography, between £500 and £10,000 an acre.

With commercial forestry there is no tax on harvested timber and no capital gains tax on the growth of its value. In another tax break, woodland is exempt from inheritance tax as long as the buyer lives at least two years from the time of the investment.

Commercial investors typically hand over a minimum of £100,000 for forests, but those without such deep pockets can buy a tax-efficient slice through a special forest fund with a layout of as little as £10,000.

Returns on woodland funds have previously grown by about 5% a year, according to the Investment Property Databank Forestry Index.

LAST MARCH OF THE ENTS

The oldest tree in the world is a spruce in Sweden that took root more than 9500 years ago, soon after the close of the ice age. The trunk can last 600 years, but the roots do not die. The most ancient tree in Britain is the Fortingall Yew near Aberfeldy, Tayside, some 5000-years-old. The 1000-year-old Major Oak in Sherwood Forest, Nottinghamshire, is big enough to shelter many Merry Men.

Ancient woodland – more than 400 years old – covers less than 2% of Great Britain, and the vast majority of these trees are in small pockets no more than 50 acres in size. Over the past century the amount of ancient woodland has more than halved and 46 broadleaved woodland species have become extinct.

Most commercial forests are Sitka spruce, as broadleaved deciduous woodland is not generally such a good investment, taking up to a hundred years to mature. However, deciduous can still be an investment if the land grows in value – and there is the added bonus of being able to enjoy your own idyllic retreat.

Prices for pockets of private woodland typically start at £15,000.

The Forestry Commission offers grants to plant new woods, manage and improve existing ones, and restock harvested woodland with replacement trees.

Although private woodland retreats can provide a great place for camping, family adventures or simple escape, planning permission must be granted for any buildings and only storage sheds are usually allowed.

Buyers have a responsibility not to neglect or destroy woodland, and no more than 12 full-grown trees can be cut down without a Forestry Commission license.

 ## SEE THE WOOD FOR THE TREES

Further information is available from Forestry Commission (www.forestry.gov.uk). Outfits that provide advice and trading markets for woodland purchases include www.woodlands.co.uk, and chartered surveyors John Clegg & Co (www.johnclegg.co.uk); and UPM Tilhill (www.upm-tilhill.com). Forest land and fund providers include Fountains Forestry (www.fountainsforestry.co.uk); and Forestry Investment Management, (www.fimltd.co.uk).

World War Paraphernalia

The Great War shaped the modern world and few people's ancestors were not touched by the terrible conflict. It is therefore of little surprise that this era tends to attract most attention among collectors and investors in global conflict paraphernalia.

As time passes there is also a growing interest in history relating to World War II. There are a huge range of artefacts relating to this and other wars, and they are always in demand. Shared interest with other adventurous investors, and research, are important parts of this collecting.

The futility of World War I was only realised afterwards. At the time, volunteers across the country eagerly queued to join the army and 'bash the Boche'. Propaganda embodying this spirit and the national call by Lord Kitchener ('Your Country Needs You') are now some of the most highly sought after pieces of history.

Typical is Savile Lumley's famous 1915 portrait of a man next to a child holding a toy soldier, the little boy asking: 'Daddy, what did you do in the war?' It could be picked up for £250 about 15 years ago but now costs at least £600.

The cap badges and medals from long-disbanded regiments – including WW1 "pals battalions" of regional groups – have unique nostalgia appeal as collectables, and can go for up to £300. Be wary, though, in a market flooded with forgeries.

Even regular service medals that were seen as fairly worthless until recently will now cost £100. Gallantry medals from any conflict sell for thousands of pounds. (See also the entry on *Medals*.)

The khaki WW1 Tommy uniform is an iconic piece of kit and tunics fetch £500 to £1000, depending on condition. However, trousers fetch more than £2000, as they are rarer. After the war they were still useful, and most got worn out on Civvy Street.

The tin helmet only arrived in 1915, when it was realised that shrapnel protection was required. The earliest examples go for £500. These replaced the rare "gor' blimey" soft cap – as nicknamed by sergeant majors – now worth up to £1500.

Across the trenches the Hun wore stylish spike-laden headgear. A WWI Prussian officer's pickelhaube is a collectors' favourite and the best-condition examples can sell for £2000.

World War II uniform is also popular, but thanks to more examples surviving items can still be picked up for a few hundred pounds. Commando and Paratrooper clothing, though – both of which formed in 1940 – sells for much more.

 DON'T MENTION THE WAR

Nazi costumes and artefacts are among the most collectable of all militaria. However, as fascist memorabilia they should be treated with caution. Although of great historic interest, they attract unwanted attention and are not always viewed as socially acceptable. The swastika logo can still offend.

A soldier's best friend is his rifle. Keeping soldiers company throughout World War I and also much of the Second was the trusty "smelly" – Short Magazine Lee Enfield (SMLE). So many of these warhorses were produced that they can still be purchased for between £250 and £350 – deactivated, of course.

If you fancy something bigger, why not invest in a military vehicle? A US WW2 Willys Jeep can be picked up for £8000, while the starting price for a German Sherman tank is about £50,000. Check you have enough room in the garage.

 FILLING THE WAR CHEST

Guidebooks include (again) *Tommy's War: British Military Memorabilia, 1914-1918*, by Peter Doyle; *The Home Front: British Wartime Memorabilia, 1939-1945*, by Peter Doyle and Paul Evans. Magazine *Gun Mart* provides details of militaria traders and trade fairs. See also, for military vehicles, www.milweb.net.

About the Author

Toby Walne is an award-winning national journalist who specialises in alternative investments. A writer for the *Mail on Sunday* he also regularly contributes to other newspapers and is a magazine columnist.

Toby was first kicked out the office more than a decade ago and told not to return until he had a story. He has rarely been back in since.

In search of adventure and stories Toby has motorcycled from John o'Groats to Land's End, visited the war zones of Afghanistan and Iraq, climbed up Mount Kenya and taken numerous trains through Swindon and Doncaster.

Acknowledgements

Dr Livingstone and those who share his spirit of adventure. Jeff Prestridge, personal finance editor at the *Mail on Sunday*, for inspiration, guidance and support. Deputy editor Richard Dyson and his ability to study facts. Jo Thornhill and Stephen Womack for financial wisdom and toleration. *The Financial Mail* editor Lisa Buckingham, and economics editor Dan Atkinson for telling me to write a book about post offices. *Moneywise* editor Rachel Lacey and all those that have helped me learn of strange ways to make money over the years, including Patrick Collinson at the *Guardian*. Ian Donaldson of the *Northants Evening Telegraph* and a homeless man in Japan. Also thanks for ideas and material to Paul Evans and Julian Walker and the Harriman House team for their enthusiasm and willingness to humour me along the way.

The majority of the illustrations used were sourced through Dover Publications, www.doverpublications.com, with some from www.istockphoto.com, but many others were sourced individually, so I would also like to say thank you to the following people for their help in suggesting and supplying images; Michel Snoeck for help with Rupert, Paul Harrison at Miscellanea, www.brokenbog.com, Simon Kirby at Thomas Crapper & Co. Ltd, www.thomas-crapper.com, Bruce Charles Skilbeck at Poster Classics Sarl, www.posterclassics.com, John Hayes and his campervan at www.motornstuffart.co.uk, Debra Gavant with the shrunken head at www.debragavant.com, Simon Terry at Anglepoise Ltd, www.anglepoise.com, Louise Reynolds at Stanley Gibbons Limited, www.stanleygibbons.com and Bob Shaver for advice on Monopoly. Acknowledgements of copyright to Iain McClumpha © 1996, Dalek design © BBC 1963. Dalek concept © estate of Terry Nation 1963. And the airship came from the September, 1929 issue of *Meccano Magazine*.